Wonderful Ways
TO **LOVE**
A **GRANDCHILD**

Also by Judy Ford:

Wonderful Ways to Love a Child

Wonderful Ways to Be a Family

Wonderful Ways to Love a Teen

Expecting Baby

Between Mother & Daughter

JUDY
FORD

Wonderful Ways
TO LOVE
A GRANDCHILD

Foreword by
Sue Patton Thoele

Conari
Press

This edition first published in 2006 by
Red Wheel/Weiser, LLC
With offices at:
500 Third Street, Suite 230
San Francisco, CA 94107
www.redwheelweiser.com

ISBN-10: 1-57324-294-2
ISBN-13: 978-1-57324-294-3

Library of Congress Cataloging-in-Publication Data
Ford, Judy, 1944–
Wonderful ways to love a grandchild/Judy Ford; foreword by Sue Patton Thoele
p.   cm.
ISBN 1-57324-097-4 (alk. paper)
1. Grandparenting.   2. Grandparents.   3. Grandparent and child.   I. Title.
HQ759.9.F67   1997
306.874'5—dc21   97-17044

Typeset in Bembo by Maija Tollefson

Printed in Canada
TCP

10   9   8   7   6   5   4   3   2   1

JUDY
FORD

Wonderful Ways
TO LOVE
A GRANDCHILD

Foreword by
Sue Patton Thoele

Conari
Press

This edition first published in 2006 by
Red Wheel/Weiser, LLC
With offices at:
500 Third Street, Suite 230
San Francisco, CA 94107
www.redwheelweiser.com

ISBN-10: 1-57324-294-2
ISBN-13: 978-1-57324-294-3

Library of Congress Cataloging-in-Publication Data
Ford, Judy, 1944–
Wonderful ways to love a grandchild/Judy Ford; foreword by Sue Patton Thoele
p.   cm.
ISBN 1-57324-097-4 (alk. paper)
1. Grandparenting. 2. Grandparents.   3. Grandparent and child.   I. Title.
HQ759.9.F67   1997
306.874'5—dc21   97-17044

Typeset in Bembo by Maija Tollefson

Printed in Canada
TCP

10 9 8 7 6 5 4 3 2 1

For my mother, Phyllis Sorensen,
who is always willing to be there for her granddaughter Amanda;
in so doing, she is also there for me.
And in memory of my father, Wally Sorensen,
who was our protector.

Grandparenting
is a gift
between two people
at opposite ends
of their journey.

Wonderful Ways to Love a Grandchild

Connection

Courage

Foreword

GRANDPARENTING IS JUST THAT—GRAND! Those of you who are already grandparents know exactly what I mean, and those of you who have grandparenting to look forward to are in for a soul-altering treat.

Between grandparent and grandchild there exists the rare opportunity to express and receive unconditional love. Both generations, relieved of obligation and expectation, are free to fully appreciate and delight in each other as individuals. This accepting love between grandparent and grandchild provides a safe sanctuary in which the inner core of our being can feel safe to shine brightly and freely.

For about two weeks following the blessing of being present at my grandson's birth, I experienced "continual tear trickle." I cried while holding Josh, while thinking or talking about him, and even when I wasn't consciously aware of him at all. In retrospect, I think that the mystery and wonder of birth was something that I was absorbing much better as a grandmother than I had as a young mom. At twenty-two I was mostly terrified and insecure in my role. At fifty-seven I was, and continue to be, awestruck and saturated with gratitude.

Wonderful Ways to Love a Grandchild is a useful book for both veteran grandparents and grandparents-in-waiting because it underscores the valuable contributions we can make to our grandchildren's lives just by being our authentic selves. Judy Ford not only gives us wonderful ways to love a grandchild, but also provides grandparents with ample insights regarding aging gracefully, graciously, and, perhaps, a little outrageously. By pointing out the ways in which grandparents and grandchildren are gifts to one another, the author helps each of us claim the riches inherent in our "grand" relationships.

One of the most precious gifts grandchildren give to grandparents is to help us lighten up and relax our tight grasp on "concrete reality," thereby becoming open to mystery, magic, and awe. The first smile I ever received from my infant grandson, for example, was in answer to my question, "So, Honey, will you introduce me to the fairies, elves, and angels when you get a little older?" Even though Josh supposedly wasn't old enough to smile, his little lips curled up in a wonderful recognition that looked exactly like a smile to me. "Yes," he seemed to promise, "I will help you regain the intuition and imagination of your youth."

From the purity of newness and the wisdom of experience, grandchildren and grandparents bridge the years. Very often they share a recognition that there are heart and soul connections which transcend the limitations of both ends of the aging spectrum. After I had been away on a trip for two weeks, ten-month-old Josh cleverly and clearly communicated to me without the benefit of words. I wondered if he would remember me, and as we were rocking and gazing into each other's eyes at naptime, I asked—not aloud, but telepathically from my heart—if he remembered Grammy. Smiling, he took his pacifier out of his mouth and put the non-nipple end up to my mouth and then grabbed for it as I twisted my head around just out of his reach. I was delighted because it was a game that we'd made up about a month before and I'd forgotten.

Although I was satisfied that he did remember me, he still had another reassurance for me and wiggle-wormed until I put him on the floor. Quick as a wink he scooted over to his book shelf and pulled out a purple book entitled *Naptime is Laptime.* As I read the last line, I knew without a shadow of a doubt that this little one had read my heart's question and was answering brilliantly within the limitations of his body. The line? "But the very best place for naptime is Grandma's lap." Wow!

Children are so much wiser than we give them credit for. One task we grandparents have is to widen our view and credit the shining souls loaned to us with being wisdom holders, light bearers, and unconditional love dispensers. Gurus in diapers.

They can help us regain our freedom, and we can help them retain theirs. From talking with other grandparents, I don't believe I'm alone in feeling that my grandson and I share a certain mystical freedom. Josh is filled with the freedom of unlimited possibility, spontaneity, curiosity, and wonder, accompanied by an absolute belief that his needs are important. Being with him fills me with hope about the ongoing process of regaining my own once innate sense of endless promise, reverence, and self-worth. He has become my teacher. And I, hopefully, am his also.

According to William Wordsworth, ". . . trailing clouds of glory do we come from God, who is our home: Heaven lies about us in our infancy! . . . " Assuming the poet is correct, our children come to us wrapped in the fragrance and glory of God's love. As people of grandparenting age, we are probably in the process of reconnecting with the clouds of glory from which we came and toward which we are moving. How wonderful when grandchild and grandparent can intertwine these twin strands of glory and exuberantly indulge in an appreciative and joyous dance of love.

I know that you will enjoy and benefit from the wise guidance and practical dance steps found in Judy Ford's excellent book, *Wonderful Ways to Love a Grandchild*.

—**Sue Patton Thoele**, author of *The Courage to Be Yourself, Heart Centered Marriage,* and *The Woman's Book of Spirit*

The Gift of Grandparenting

Open your heart to your grandchild,
and your days will suddenly fill with
moments of gladness and delight.
No bands will be marching, no
trumpets will be blaring, so wake up
and pay close attention,or the gifts
they're bringing might quietly slip
out of sight.

Jim sat on the couch, reading the newspaper as four-year-old Parker climbed up next to him and said, "Grandpa, wha'cha doing?"

"Reading the paper," Jim answered. Parker looked up at Grandpa, and Jim looked down at Parker. For a moment, there was silence, then Jim went back to reading. Parker climbed down and Jim asked, "Where are you going?"

"To get a book." Book in hand, Parker climbed back onto the couch, snuggled very close to Grandpa, and started looking at pages.

"Is that a good book?" Jim asked.

"Yeah," nodded Parker. And they both continued reading.

Such a sweet and simple moment—an ordinary moment—yet in an instant I could see the love shining on their faces.

Make no mistake about it: Grandparents and grandchildren share something special. The relationship is a virtual lovefest of the most splendid kind. Just ask any grandparent about their grandchild and notice the look on his or her face. It's not an everyday look—it's a soulful one, a look of joy, of pride, of recognition. It's love at first sight, for grandparents and grandchildren seem to recognize something in each other that is intangible yet ever-present. Perhaps it is innocence that they recognize in each other. The innocence of youth meeting the innocence of age. Or maybe it is the wisdom of the very young encountering the wisdom of the elderly.

Grandkids and grandparents have an understanding, a special way of communicating, a sixth sense. When I ask grandparents to tell me about their grandchildren, they're eager and more than willing, but they look upon me with pity, and I can tell they're thinking: *She can't possibly understand—she's not a grandmother.* And when I ask kids what they like about their grandparents, they look at me, shaking their heads with such suspicion that I can tell they're convinced it's a ridiculous question. They're too polite to say it, but they seem to be thinking to themselves: *Isn't it enough that I like my grandmother? Does she have to know the particulars?*

All the grandparents I speak with want to give their grandchildren something—pass on something, teach something, leave something—but they can't quite decide on what that something is. *Wonderful Ways to Love a Grandchild* is about what you are giving and what you are receiving in your grandparenting, about how to enhance the experience so that you can offer the fullness of who you are and receive the depth of love from your grandchildren in return.

This connection is important, for grandparenting is a gift for both you and your grandchildren. Your paths have crossed for a reason. Indeed, this little book is filled with true stories of grandparents and grandchildren who, by divine destiny, are offering one another hope and optimism, understanding and compassion. They give each other a view of the world that might otherwise be missed. Smiling, cuddling, bragging about your grandchildren—all have a significant purpose for both generations. Let this book guide you as you uncover the magnitude of what you are giving and receiving.

Wonderful Ways to Love a Grandchild is divided into three sections which reflect the three aspects of grandparenting—*clarity, connection,* and *courage.*

To grandparent well means to love without conditions, to love for the sake of your grandchild. With clarity of vision, you come to know yourself well enough that you're able to give to your grandchild what no one else can—the things of life that truly matter.

The second section is about the heart connection that unites a family. It focuses on ways that you can foster depth in your relationship that satisfies and benefits not only you and your grandchild, but your adult children as well; for it is difficult to have a good relationship with your grandchildren if you are estranged from their parents.

The third section is about growing and going forward—making the best choices for the sake of your entire family—for oftentimes it is only with the maturity of age that we can see what is needed for our families.

I'm not a grandparent, but I'm old enough to be, and I've had plenty of life experience—birth of a child, death of a husband, the full range of joy and grief. Many of my friends and clients are grandparents, and they often ask my opinion on how to best foster loving relationships with their adult children and grandchildren, which I think qualifies me as a member of the "grand generation." I've watched them with their grandchildren enough to know that grandparenting is a splendid obsession with dividends. Loving a grandchild comes naturally. Honoring the love and knowing how to receive it, taking it all in, and enjoying it is quite another thing.

Wonderful Ways to Love a Grandchild is not just about your grandchild—it's also about you. Grandparents in our society are more involved with their grandchildren today than they were in the past, even when the "extended family" is extended all right—often clear across the country. Although a greater number of grandparents live in separate cities today than in previous generations, they are more involved with their grandchildren: telephoning, communicating through letters and e-mail, and flying and driving cross-country to visit. And more and more grandparents are now the primary caregivers of children because of both parents working outside the home. There is also a rise in the number of grandparents living with their children and grandchildren.

Many of these changes in the traditional role of grandparents are a reflection of changes in our ever-evolving society as a whole. Modern technology makes long-distance communication and travel more accessible and convenient for everyone. And with the baby boomers now having grandbabies of their own, grandparents constitute a larger sector of our population than ever before. Grandparents today are healthier, living longer, and have more money—much of which they are spending on their grandchildren.

As we boomers move into the grand generation, we still have personal issues to consider. We're anxious about who we are and what we want to do. We're asking questions about what life will be like for us now that we are aging. And as with all life passages, there are personal adjustments to be made, fears and unfulfilled longings to be faced. As we turn over parenting to the next generation, we search for ways to fill the void.

As you reflect on where you've been and where you're going, let *Wonderful Ways to Love a Grandchild* direct you back to the precious moments that bring you so much joy. No sound is sweeter than the voice of your grandchild calling: "Hi, Grandma . . . hi, Grandpa." Listen closely. It's enough to make your body tingle, give you goose bumps, put a smile on your face, and add a spring to your step. The meaning is clear: Someone is genuinely reaching out to you. Thank the heavens for the healing sound! Doubts and worries vanish; you can mull over the big issues later. Right now, you're busy with more important matters—your grandchild is in your midst! *Wonderful Ways to Love a Grandchild* invites you to treasure and nurture the sweetness of this precious and most uncomplicated relationship.

Clarity

Many years from now when your grandchildren are grown and have children of their own, they will reminisce and tell stories about you, unlocking a tiny time capsule of love energy flooding their souls with sweet memories.

Be very clear, don't stop growing, stay in the flow of life.

Respect Your Life Experience

Perhaps you've noticed that people are starting to recognize you as an elder, an honored and respected member of your family. You wonder sometimes if it's because your age is showing. Although age may qualify you for senior citizen discounts, it's not what qualifies you to be a grandparent. That requires maturity.

A mature grandparent has the wisdom to acknowledge the challenges and heartaches of life so that he or she can appreciate the blessings, joy, and laughter. Maturity is marked by inner integrity, honesty, and goodness. It's knowing that you alone are responsible for your life. You don't blame others. You accept responsibility for your own happiness. If you're down in the dumps, you don't stay there long, because you know that life has a way of working out. If you've messed up, you admit it. You're not defeated by mistakes, but rather keep on living and trying again and again.

Maturity is the ability to enjoy the unexpected and roll with the punches. That's the wisdom that is truly beneficial to your grandchildren. Children are inundated with far too many examples of adults blaming their circumstances on bad luck, the stars, the weather, their parents, or "the other guy." Children need examples of people behaving responsibly, living happily, and making the most of their circumstances. Children will make mistakes, have setbacks, and experience disappointments—it's part of growing up. You can't protect them from frustrations, nor should you. But with your shining example, they can gain an understanding of what it means to accept responsibility for creating a wonderful life.

By watching you face your challenges, they'll learn that they too have what it takes to face life's ups and downs. They'll discover that through perseverance and determination they can succeed. You're a living testament to durability and goodness. That's the maturity you offer: a mixture of experience and a heart full of acceptance. The gift you can bestow on your grandchildren is a strong sense of self and a respect for life as a continuous journey.

Margaret was such a grandma. In spite of her few chances to spend long periods of time with her grandchildren, they were nevertheless taken with her pluck and true grit. In her later years, she had debilitating back problems and suffered bouts of agonizing pain. Although she acknowledged her health problems when asked, she never focused on her misery when her grandchildren were with her. Instead, she took delight in hearing about their lives. She conveyed to them a generosity of soul and a fighting spirit. She taught them that you can't always choose what happens in life, but you can choose where to put your focus.

You're a master! You've seen and done many things over the course of your long life. You've survived heartaches and setbacks, and you've celebrated loves and victories. You've learned from living, and you've probably gained more common sense than you ever thought you'd need. You've gained the seasoning that comes with age, and your grandchildren are the beneficiaries.

Let Your Grandness Shine

Webster's defines *grand* as:

Large and impressive in size, scope, or extent; magnificent. Rich and sumptuous. Of a solemn, stately, or splendid nature. Dignified or noble in appearance or effect. Noble or admirable in conception or intent. Lofty or sublime in character. Wonderful or very pleasing. Having higher rank than others of the same category. Having more importance than others; principal.

Now that's certainly a lot to live up to, but it doesn't need to scare you. You *are* grand, and this is the time in your life to let it show, not in a bragging or boastful way but rather simply by your character. Your grandchildren know you through your personality, your disposition, and your mannerisms. It's not so much what you do as who you are. To be grand, you don't have to do anything more than be yourself. You don't have to lecture, advise, reprimand, scold, or coach. This is another benefit of being a *grand*parent rather than the primary parent.

If you've ever been to a redwood forest and walked among the three-thousand-year-old trees, you will never again doubt the grandeur of an aged creature. Walking among the three-hundred-foot Sequoias, I'm in awe, talking only in whispers. It's as though I'm standing in a splendid cathedral. A reverence for the natural order and progression of life prevails. The rings of the tree trunk denote the age of the tree—the more rings, the older the tree. Those of us fortunate enough to live, and strong enough to survive, eventually become old. Like the rings of a redwood tree, let your age proudly show your status. Your "rings" show how far you've come. They're your emblem of subsistence and strength.

You've lived long enough to be a grandparent, but that doesn't mean you're "over the hill." Research has shown that senior citizens are not doomed to years of infirmity, decrepitude, senility, or degradation. Quite the contrary: With exercise, good nutrition, a positive attitude, and a sense of humor, your life can be full of vitality, enthusiasm, and adventure.

The grandparenting years can be spectacular, and we're the torch bearers of what these years can be. The middle and younger generations need examples of how to live fully; they're following in your footsteps, looking to you to show them the way. Someday they too might be grandparents and, if you've been steadfast on your course, they will look forward to it. So be as grand as a redwood and remember that in the eyes of your grandchild, you already are.

Define Your Grandparenting Philosophy

Whether you're an eager, "I can hardly wait" grandma or a reluctant, "I'm not sure I'm ready" type, you need to think about the kind of grandparent you want to be. How much time do you want to devote to your role? What do you want to give your grandchildren? What do you want them to think and feel about you?

There seem to be two stereotypical notions of grandparents. On one extreme are the doting, waiting, loving, all-caring, and sentimental grandparents "without a life of their own." On the other extreme is the interfering, bossy, take-charge, "I know what's right for you" stereotype. Becoming a grandparent is a defining moment, but you don't have to adopt a stereotypical role. You can still be *you*, but you need to grapple with what that means.

Your outlook on grandparenting probably came from your own grandparents, so it is helpful to think about them as you develop your philosophy. Did you know your grandparents? Were you close to them? How much time did you spend with them? What do you remember about those times? What kind of grandparents were *your* parents to *your* children?

Since my friend Jean became a grandmother, she's full of recollections. She remembers her father, John Lundstrom, who used to carry candy in his pocket. It got his grandsons to always ask, "Wha'cha got in your pocket?" He also kept it in a jar by his bed, in case he got a midnight craving.

Jean says, "Of course, my boys thought that must be another one of those 'for adults only' privileges, denied to them, which made them yearn to mature quickly."

Perhaps you might like to write a grandparenting mission statement. If you already have grandchildren, think about your relationship with them. Do you enjoy them? Do you look forward to being with them? How much time do you spend together? Is it enough or would you prefer more? Is there anything you can do to improve your relationship with the children or their parents? Because there are no classes on grandparenting, you'll have to chart your own course. Lynne and Mike agree: "In adjusting to this new role, we know all the things we *don't* want to do or be like, but we're not so clear on the 'what to do.'"

Your grandparenting philosophy is a reflection of your love and commitment to family in general and grandchildren in particular. Your philosophy will keep you focused on what is important to you in your relationship with your grandchildren. By putting your philosophy into practice, you take an active role in forming an alliance with your grandchild.

Appreciate Wrinkles

My seventy-five-year-old mother says that there are two ways to tell when you're getting older: (1) by looking in the mirror and (2) when you start putting rubber bands around everything. I know I'm fitting into the dignitary category because (1) when strangers learn my age they frequently say, "You don't look that old," or they nod in recognition as if they're thinking, Yep. I thought so and (2) I have a rubber band around my checkbook.

Recently, I've begun to notice advertisements in the *Seattle Times* for cosmetic surgery, promising that "you'll feel better if you look younger"—all it takes is a tummy tuck, a face peel, a lid reduction, or a facelift. If I'm willing to pay a small fortune and go under the knife, I can look better than I did at forty. I might be tempted to call a plastic surgeon if I looked in the mirror more than twice a day, but since I don't like anesthesia and recovery rooms, I've decided to keep busy instead. I have too much to do—there are classes to take, beaches to comb, back roads to explore, countries to visit. Besides, I'm starting to truly appreciate lines on my face.

All seasons are beautiful and so are all faces, whether fresh and smooth or weathered and wrinkled. An old person who has lived life fully is beautiful. It isn't beauty potions, liposuction, or hair replacement that gives an elder beauty—it's living life to the fullest. Trying to look young makes an older person look odd, artificial, and contrived. Our society's obsession with youth sends a contradictory message to our grandchildren: We say, "respect your elders," yet we elders strive desperately to look anything but.

Aging is as natural as the seasons. Wrinkles, graying hair, and a softer, sagging body show that you've had a long journey and have in many ways mastered the art of living. Now you're putting your energy into facing the challenges of aging with dignity. We all know that we live in a youth culture and that it is therefore hard to grow old gracefully. But there are hopeful signs that aging is becoming more socially acceptable. As baby boomers age, society is beginning to recognize the value that comes with life experience.

Our grandchildren can help us accept our aging, because children aren't easily fooled by looks. Rather, they see our inner beauty. Janet, a beauty consultant for more than thirty-five years and the proud grandmother of five-year-old Jacob, says, "Believe me, I know about beauty, and this face is out of its prime. But when Jacob pats my face and says, 'I kiss your beautiful face,' I'm not concerned about the fountain of youth because I'm getting unconditional love."

A person desperately clinging to some long-gone moment is a not a pretty sight. But when a man or woman accepts old age as natural, you can't find a more beautiful face than an old one— wrinkled through many seasons, seasoned through many experiences, matured and all grown up.

Prepare for Adjustments

Just when you thought you had parenting conquered, you become a grandparent and suddenly see your own child from a whole new perspective. My friend Jean describes it well:

When we landed in Helsinki, where my son Todd lives, I looked around for him while we were waiting in Customs. Finally, I saw him on the other side of the glass, waving. He was bundled up in a thick jacket with a hood, so I didn't see what he was holding in his arms until we got out in the lobby. Nestled down deep in his arms, amid the pile of blankets, was a tiny pink little face—that's all. I was speechless. I had been informed about everything from prenatal visits to the birth itself, and I repeatedly fantasized about all of this, but it wasn't until that moment that I understood what had taken place. It wasn't just the miracle of this baby, but the recognition that *my* baby—this six-foot-tall young man—had some how matured to a degree far beyond the point his little mother saw him. Coming to terms with that is something I'm still working on. I am totally fascinated with his relationship with his baby, Emma. Todd is a beautiful father. He comes by it so naturally and so easily. This touches me and gives me much joy.

I am in love with being a grandmother and having this beautiful being, Emma, in my life. Although Emma's existence is not for me, I am very thankful to Todd and Reija for her. I also miss my child, however. I miss being needed as a mother by him. I know that this part of my life is over, but it was so defining of who I was. It doesn't peel off easily.

Nothing prepares you for the breathtaking moment when you see your child—who in some ways is still your baby—holding, cuddling, and caring for a little human being. Once you took care of his every need; now he's doing the same for another. In a instant, you recognize that your role in your child's life is evolving, and it catches you off-guard. You're no longer the primary caregiver, and you're not sure who you are in relation to your child. You know you're needed, but you're not sure how or when. Learning to relate to this new image of your child can be more formidable than grandparenting. It will take a little time and that's okay.

"You're telling the grandparents to butt out of the child-rearing advice, aren't you?" Ginger asked me. She says, "I remember having to sit my mother down and tell her that just because I was raising my children differently didn't mean that I thought she was a bad mother. That one honest conversation alleviated a lot of problems between us."

The evolution of your relationship with your child doesn't negate the past or lessen the love. It just puts it in a different ball park. As Jean says, "I know this is where it belongs; I guess I'm getting there too."

Trust Yourself in Transition

If you're wondering how you fit into your family now that your kids are parents themselves; if you're feeling slightly out of step because your identity is changing and you're not sure where to put your energies; if you're thinking about selling the family home so you can travel more lightly—you're in the midst of a life passage, moving through one more developmental phase. When you're struggling to find a new direction, while reminiscing over the past, it's a bittersweet time; remember that it's not the first time you've been caught in momentary limbo.

Remember when your five-year-old daughter rode off on the school bus for the first time, waving good-bye as you cried at the curb? Walking home, you wondered if your little girl needed you anymore. The morning hours dragged; restless, you paced from room to room and drank too much coffee. You taught her to ride a trike and bought her first bicycle; then, seemingly overnight, she was driving your car. Where did the time go? Once she was your baby; now she's someone's mother.

Passing from one phase of life to another is the natural human cycle, yet when your transition is in midwinter, before the spring buds unfold, there are moments when life is at a standstill. The ground is frozen and you're retreating inward, less active, more quiet, whirling with memories of where you've been and wondering where life will take you next. You're looking back and also looking forward, perhaps anxious, agitated, yet surprisingly peaceful and still.

You've faced loss before, and have been entangled by the bewilderment of *What now?* You're mulling it over, and you'll figure it out. You've done it before and you'll do it again. It's the exhilaration of self-discovery that propels each beginning. It's a rite of passage. You've always found your way before, and you will again.

After Jim died of cancer, Maggie decided to sell the big house and move to a condo. "My daughters-in-law packed the boxes, my sons moved the furniture, my grandkids supervised the garage sale, and I cried," she said.

"I thought it was best for me to move, but I didn't think I would survive. For forty-two years I'd been someone's wife, but on moving day I was just a single person with my own individual life. For about nine months, I wandered aimlessly until I figured out that this was my time to do exactly what I wanted to. And so I am. I work two days a week at a florist shop, I'm indulging my passion for growing African violets, and I am making new friends."

From one stage in life, you pass to another. Trust yourself to do it well—your grandchildren are watching.

Rejoice in the Endless Possibilities

Whether you're becoming a grandparent for the first or tenth time, you're bound to encounter emotional challenges as you pass from one stage of life to another. The challenges can be intense, because grandparenthood often coincides with retirement, menopause, moving out of the family home, or other such major life changes.

Needless to say, the transition from parenthood to grandparenthood is not always easy or smooth. You've spent twenty or more years being an active parent, and now you've gone from full house to empty nest in what seems like a few short days. On the one hand, there is the fulfillment of watching your daughter become a loving mother, yet there is also the ache of feeling left out of her new family. Seeing your little girl with a baby in her arms brings incredible joy, yet you wonder what's next in life for you.

We face many endings as we approach our later years. Although there is grief with these passings, you can make the losses easier to bear by focusing on the possibilities inherent in this time of your life. You have fewer responsibilities, demands, and pressures. You have more freedom to pursue your dreams. You have more time to explore your untapped creative potential, to do the things you've always wanted to try. You can be spontaneous and follow your own rhythms—sleep in late, get up early, eat when you're hungry; you can volunteer, plant a garden, make a career change, go to the movies in the afternoon, or join the Peace Corps!

Liza brags about her grandmother Letha, who is enrolling in college to study history—just because she likes it. Chloe, an artist who enjoys dressing the part, is tickled when her eight-year-old granddaughter asks, "When you come visit us, Grandma, will you wear your gypsy dress?" On Chloe's last visit, her granddaughter took her to school for show and tell.

You have the insight to appreciate what truly matters to you and, with that wisdom, you can have a wonderful relationship with your grandchild. Whatever your personal focus, your enthusiasm is invaluable to a child. Annie, a great-grandmother of five, advises, "I stopped looking for meaning at this stage of my life. I want to have fun and enjoy everything—that's enough for me."

Whether your approach is philosophical, practical, or lighthearted, remember that children blessed with grandparents who are filled with the energy of possibility get a positive view of life. It's inspiring to see people enjoying their lives no matter what age; it fills you with optimism, and that is a legacy every child needs.

Fancy Your New Name

As soon as you catch your breath after hearing that earth-moving announcement—"You're going to be a grandparent"—you're likely to begin pondering names. Not baby names—that's the parents' prerogative—but grandparent names. What will your grandchild call you?

Claire wasn't thrilled about becoming a grandmother and couldn't fathom being called by such a title in public. "After all" she said, "I'm only forty-three years old." Every time her daughter-in-law referred to her as "Grandma," Claire rolled her eyes and sighed. Then a stranger said, "You don't look old enough to be a grandmother"; and from then on, Claire found unequivocal pride when boasting, "This is my grandson!"

Kaye was so enthralled with being a first-time grandmother that she didn't care what her new title might be. When her granddaughter was old enough to get the words out, she christened Kaye "Gana-K," and everyone has followed suit.

There are many grand names to consider, from the traditional *Grandma, Nana, Nanny, Grandpa, Pop,* and *Papa* to a newfangled one like *Ma Ma Grand,* bestowed on Irene by her three-year-old granddaughter. Friends and relatives agree that *Ma Ma Grand* fits her to a tee, and that's exactly how she wants any future grandchildren to know her. Dorothy liked *Honey ma* and wasn't shy about letting the entire family know that that was her new name. Barbara chose Grammy, and Margaret became

Mimi. Madeline carried on her French heritage and was called *Grand-mère*. Of Norwegian background, Olga was given the name *Mormor* by her twelve very American grandchildren and great-grandchildren. Manuel is *Abuelo* to his twenty-one grandchildren.

Some families use the traditional *Grandma* or *Grandpa* for both sides of the family, adding the first name such as *Grandma Helen* or *Grandpa Joe*. This reserves the more formal and traditional *Grandmother* and *Grandfather* for the great-grandparents. If you design a one-of-a-kind name for yourself, just make sure it's user-friendly—meaning that a two year old can pronounce it. And remember: As these stories show, sometimes your grandchildren take the matter into their own hands.

Sandra said, "Any name my grandchildren call me is music to my ears, but I don't like it when my husband calls me 'Grandma'—I'm not *his* grandma!" Once you become a grandparent, often your own kids start calling you by your new name, and that can take some real getting use to.

Regardless of what you choose to be called or what name you are given, your new name becomes a testament of your special relationship to a child. Your grand-moniker is a label of love, representing sweet and trusting affection. Your name is more than just a tag—it's a term of endearment, a sign that you forever hold a special place in the heart of a child.

Marie, fondly known as *Nana Re*, says, "My heart melts when I hear my name, because their voices are full of so much love." The sound of love is your grandchild calling, "Come here, Grammakee," or "Can I ride with you, Grandpa?" You'll never hear a more heartwarming sound.

Embark on Your Spiritual Journey

You are a spiritual being on a spiritual journey. If you haven't already started on your path, you can't put it off any longer. It's time to wake up spiritually and turn your will over to the highest good—not just for your own sake, but for your children's children and their children whom you may never get to meet. You are a crucial role model for future generations. Unless you uncover the spiritual part of your being, your life will be shallow, and your grandchildren may grow up rootless and obsessed only with material gain.

What does it mean to wake up spiritually? It means to be willing to keep learning, to allow every situation to teach you to love more deeply. You can learn something about yourself from every life experience, or you can brush the opportunities aside and remain spiritually immature, convincing yourself that you already know it all. The spiritually immature person keeps inflating her ego until she's stuck in a quagmire of smugness. The spiritually mature person, on the other hand, continues to learn, softening, becoming vulnerable, allowing the force that moves the heavens to guide her. The whole of existence is working to bring you closer to the Almighty. Perhaps grandchildren are God's helpmates in charge of softening our hearts.

To walk the spiritual path means to pay attention to everything— what you are doing and where you are going. Rather than go through life on automatic pilot, you act with awareness. The more aware you are, the more you can find God everywhere. This is your greatest gift to your grandchildren and to the world.

Alice, seventy-eight, grandmother of three and great-grandmother of one, considers the years beyond seventy an unexpected treat. She says, "There is birth and death and in the middle there is living, which I am doing every day; I'm content because I have self-knowledge." She began writing poetry at the age of seventy-one because, she says, "expressing myself through poetry is my joy—it keeps me connected with my immortality."

Kenneth retired at sixty-two and started painting. "My canvas and paints keep me interested in getting up each morning and helped me discover beauty. Painting keeps my life in perspective."

Relieved from the pressures of the working world, during your grandparenting years you can express your spirit through creative pursuits that give you a deeper connection to the creative force that moves through us all. Begin your day with a prayer of rejoicing for where you've been, where you are now, and where you're going. You have within you the source of great peace; as you tap into it, your grandchildren will feel it overflowing. Life is indeed a journey. Although it's trite to say, it's definitely worth remembering. We are all traveling through life—and where you go and what you make of it is up to you.

See How Far You've Come

You've come a long way, baby! And now you get to see, feel, and rejoice in the harvest as the fruits of your labor romp in front of you. Hallelujah! It's a great day to be alive!

You've raised your kids, and hopefully they've turned out better than you. Glory be! That's the way it's supposed to be! Your kids have taken the very best of you, improved on it, and are passing that on to your grandchildren. It's the evolution of humankind right in front of your eyes. It renews your faith and gives you hope. Things are improving. You've done a fine job and you're celebrating.

You and your children have been through rough times. You've made mistakes, disagreed, fought, and come back together. You haven't always seen eye-to-eye, but now your child has presented you with a grandchild. The pain of the past is washing away as you have a common cause, a reason to get up in the morning—the child of your child is born.

Over the years, you weren't always sure of what you were doing. You asked yourself: *Am I doing enough? Am I doing too much? Am I too soft? Am I too hard?* Raising children is not easy. You worried and tried to protect them. You wondered if you were spoiling them. You tried to prepare them. You did the best you could with what you knew at the time. You've made mistakes, for sure. You've disappointed them and you've fallen short. But it doesn't matter so much anymore. Your daughter is a wonderful mother, your son a good father, and you've all come a long way.

Your children are all grown up; they've taken what you've given them, threw away what didn't fit, and added their own flavor. It's you with a twist. Now you can sigh with the satisfaction of a job well done.

"As her grandfather, I feel strong emotion whenever I see or hear her. I want the very best for her, and I want to protect her, much as I did my kids," says George of his granddaughter. "But I know that the key to her future is with my son and her mother. That's great because Jean and I get to shower her with love—and of course gifts. We also provide a strong underlying support; we are there if we are needed and feel good when asked for advice."

You've come a long way, baby! Walk tall and hold your head up high.

Be Flexible

Have you ever felt as though you're living in the middle of a movie in which the scriptwriter keeps changing his mind? Just when you think you've got your part memorized, he changes your lines. That can happen a great deal as a grandparent. You think you've got it all figured out when—wham—something comes along to shake up your world: Your daughter gets divorced and moves back home with her five-year-old son; your fifteen-year-old granddaughter is pregnant and keeping the baby. It's a surprise a minute.

Some folks go with the flow better then others, but you too can get the hang of it. The formula for success is flexibility with a dab of ingenuity and a good sense of humor mixed in. By being flexible, you're responsive to change, willing to progress with the times. Coupled with your wisdom, ingenuity, and imagination, flexibility will help you cope with any new situation. And, with a good sense of humor, even if you can't understand what the heck is going on, at least you'll be laughing.

Flexibility is the key. Whether your adult kids are working moms or stay-at-home dads, you have to be willing to understand their life choices. Parenting styles are different now than when you were raising your children, and the changes in the world your grandchildren will experience are virtually unfathomable. More than 70% of moms work outside of the home because of financial necessity; only 10% of mothers stay home full-time.

When it comes to raising children, many things have changed, but that doesn't mean you didn't do a good job with your kids. They are raising your grandchildren differently than you would—but their world is a different place. Some grandparents think that parents these days are too lenient. "I wondered if my grandkids ever ate without the television on," said one grandmother. Sharon worries that her adult children are working too much just to provide unnecessary extras: "Why does my granddaughter need her own phone?" Others are concerned because their grandchildren's lives are so rushed that the simple pleasures of childhood get jammed in between obligations, lessons, and team sports—or are lost altogether. "Don't kids play baseball in the back yard anymore?" Doug asked.

Marlene is a spontaneous "Auntie Mame" type of grandmother, and her daughter, Rachel, and son-in-law, Michael, reap the benefits of her willingness to adapt. One day before they were scheduled to fly to Tahiti on a combination business/pleasure trip, the nanny they'd hired to watch the kids quit. With only five hours' notice, Marlene changed her plans and flew from Illinois to Seattle—along with her two dogs that she never leaves behind—to step in.

A relationship with your grandchildren takes time, patience, resilience, and imagination. Be realistic in your expectations, try new approaches, stick with it—and don't forget to laugh.

Bask in the Fanfare

This is the grand generation and we're in the "in" group! That's because there are more and more of us. According to a Census Bureau study conducted between 1990 and 2000, the population of 50- to 54- year-olds increased by 55%, the largest population growth of any age group.

These are such different times than we remember our grandparents living in. We certainly don't feel or act old. We have many more years of active, healthy living to look forward to. We are no longer bound by the same stereotypes that faced our elders.

It wasn't long ago that such preposterous notions as "Old folks like to sit still" or "Sex is over at fifty" influenced how elders viewed their circumstances, bodies, and futures. But we're challenging the stereotypes and living with more enthusiasm than ever. Just look at our contemporaries: Julie Andrews, Whoopi Goldberg, Suzanne Somers— all are grandmothers. Mick Jagger and Paul Newman are grandfathers.

Oh, sure, some days you have aches and pains, yet in your heart you are incurably young; even though your body may be older, still your eyes are sparkling and as inquisitive as ever. People in the grand years are surprising themselves by saying, "Life just gets better and better," "These are the best years of my life," and "I'm happier than I've ever been."

The happiness of the grand years may be hard to describe, but you feel its freshness flowing from within your soul. The contentment that comes with age is real; it's the inner light that warms your spirit and brightens your days. With this peaceful sense of well-being, you feel invigorated, replenished. Now, perhaps for the first time, you can live life to the fullest. The newly discovered zest in the grand phase leads to a fuller expression of self. As Tom says, "Personally, I prefer to think of myself as advancing and evolving rather than aging."

Make Every Day Count

Grandparents come in all ages—the youngest I have ever met was Heather, who is thirty-six; the oldest is Deborah, who is ninety-six. Heather is raising her grandson, working as a grocery clerk, and studying design at the San Francisco Art Institute. Deborah rides the bus every day into the city to meet a friend for lunch. Patricia, who is legally blind, is the mother of seven and grandmother of twelve and has traveled to India—alone. Thorton, seventy-four, is a self-taught computer whiz who works part-time as a computer game consultant.

Grandparents today have very fascinating and diverse lifestyles. Seventy-seven-year-old Arthur, widowed for the second time, is never without female companionship. He gets free vacations as a male host on cruise ships, where he dances the night away. After her husband of forty-two years died, Linda is now living with her boyfriend. Although her kids don't like it, her grandchildren accept it, saying, "Grandma's not hurting anyone." Marilyn, fifty-nine, just purchased an elaborate three-wheel motorcycle and passed her driving test with a perfect score. Clark, age fifty-two, is indulging his love of cooking by opening a ten-table restaurant. Mike, a sixty-nine-year-old electrician, is renovating houses. Eloise, fifty-seven, is raising four grandsons on her court reporter's salary. Joyce, forty-seven, is the mother of nine-, ten-, and twenty-six-year-old sons and the grandmother of twin boys. She is currently learning sign language and teaching Sunday school.

These grandparents have hit their stride. They've had heartbreaks and bitter disappointments. They've made mistakes and had regrets. They've faced health problems and the death of loved ones, including children. They've been divorced and widowed; they've had money and been bankrupt. They look forward more often than they look back. They don't waste days pining for what might have been. Instead of brooding, they figure out what needs to be done and they do it.

To be successful, make every day count. You can do that by savoring your time alone, by staying closely connected to other people, by being physically active, and by taking care of your physical and spiritual health. The saddest thing to see is a person who has never really lived. Within you are untapped resources, rivers of potential waiting to flow. There is still a purpose in your life. If the yearning to try something new is within you, get out and try it!

Our children and grandchildren are exposed to far too many negative images of aging. They need vibrant examples of positive, attractive, healthy living at all stages of life. They need to understand that, like good wine, the human spirit gets better with age.

Address the Blues

Christina has the blues. "I'm envious of Susan because she has her grandchildren nearby. I was ready to put all my attention into the 'grandma project,' but it hasn't worked out that way. That is one way I feel like life 'got me.'"

We've all had that "life isn't working out for me" syndrome, and when you're in the middle of it, it hurts plenty. It's natural to make plans and have ideas of how we'd like our life to be. In fact, our vision for ourselves is so engrained that we often don't see any other way to live. Then when reality doesn't match our picture, we're thrown for a loop.

When Tom was growing up, he spent every Sunday afternoon running around his grandparents' farm. Fifty years later, he considers those days to be some of his best, and he looked forward to reliving those memories with his own grandchildren on his own farm. The grandkids don't see it that way. They don't come to visit often enough and they don't like riding the tractor, milking the cows, or pitching hay. Tom has learned to accept it, but he admits that he doesn't understand.

Carletta has the opposite situation. She raised her three children as a single mother, sacrificing and struggling every step of the way. The dream that kept her going was that one day she'd have time to herself to do whatever she wanted—and that didn't include taking care of kids. It hasn't worked out that way for her either. Her daughter died of AIDS, and Carletta is now the full-time guardian of three grandchildren.

Even when life is following your charted course, the blues can wash over you like a giant wave when you least expect it. You know you've got them when you're lying in bed at 3 a.m. with your eyes wide open or when you're sitting in your favorite chair watching the television with the sound turned off. You have no energy and you either have no appetite or you're eating everything in sight. You're singing, "What's it all about?"

What to do? Your reason for living is not as clear as it once was. You know you don't want to be a pest or a burden. You know your children and grandchildren love you. But in those dark nights of the soul, you're so lonely. You cry so long and hard that the only thing left is to start laughing. So you pretend to be cheerful. You say you're fine when the kids call, and you put on a smile when you're with them. Then, before you know it, you're feeling better, going out, calling your friends. You develop the philosophy *A little struggle is a must*, because you're living proof that it's through the storms that we become more grateful for our blessings.

Turn Over a New Leaf

"My grandson turned seventeen, and I'm having my second midlife crisis," Layne told me. "I was seventeen just yesterday myself, and overnight I'm over fifty-five and eligible for senior citizens' discounts. There are things I don't miss about being young, but there are plenty of things that I do—like losing weight easily and being noticed."

You've made big adjustments in every phase of your life. You've faced small and big losses. You got married, settled down, raised kids, and sent them off, and now you're facing a turning point. To you, it's a big deal—almost a crisis.

There are the obvious losses, such as a divorce or the death of a loved one, and the not-so-obvious losses, like menopause, retirement, and loss of youth. Leila's husband died the day her grandchild was born; she was in shock for a year and in mourning for another. Now she's coming out of it and facing the uphill battle of finding meaningful companionship and a new life.

"I wish I could turn over a new leaf and get on with it," Paul has been saying for eight months since he was forced into early retirement.

"After I retired," Wally jokingly tried to reassure him, "I sat in my rocking chair for the first six months; the second six months, I rocked."

Transitions are made through the emotional and spiritual process of mourning. Mourning is about rearranging your psyche and letting go of who you thought you were. It's an ache in your bones so deep that someone who hasn't been through it can't understand. It's a solitude so encompassing that you can't speak about it until you're better.

You can't get over it by buying a new outfit, taking a pill, or wishing it away. You can't drown it out by drinking. You can ignore it for a day or two, but it won't go away until you get through it. You get through it by crying, screaming, praying, and waiting. It takes doing and not doing; it takes however long it takes. You'll feel helpless and empty, fatigued and restless. You'll lack motivation, and hope will vanish. You won't seem like yourself.

If you're hurting, admit it. Kids understand these sorts of things, so there's no need to hide your sadness by pretending it isn't there. Be gentle with yourself and allow yourself to heal at your own pace.

"What's wrong, Grandpa?" asked Josh.

"I'm sad as an old hound dog," Grandpa answered.

"I'm sorry, Grandpa." And as he climbed up on Grandpa's lap, Josh said, "You can hug me if you want."

And you will heal. You'll find your way; you'll turn over a new leaf. Both you and your life will be different, but it will be okay. Expect a positive outcome—see it, plan for it, count on it. Tell your grandkids, "I'm getting better every day." And you are, because you are more independent, you are thinking clearly, and you know yourself even better. Greet the morning; jump out of bed. You've experienced loss, you've survived, and you've grown.

Live with Flair

Living with flair doesn't necessarily mean being outrageous, although if you are, your grandchildren will probably accept it more quickly than your adult kids. Living with flair means being your own person with your own unique style. It's having your own opinions and being unconcerned about what other folks may be thinking about you. It's walking to the beat of your own private drummer, getting up at the crack of dawn, and staying up all night if you want to. It's buying yourself roses and a bottle of perfume. It's taking your grandson to the art museum and to show him the Monets. It's buying temporary tattoos at the drugstore because your granddaughter wanted you to. It's going home and letting her paste one on your ankle.

If your flair is a little dull around the edges, you might try this exercise: At the top of a piece of paper, write the words *My Bliss List*. List the activities, places, things, and people that bring you joy, delight, and satisfaction. Read over your list and continue adding to it. Then, each day, little by little, design an action plan to fill your life with more and more of what is on your list.

When Caroline completed her bliss list, she knew that it was time to move closer to her grandchildren. It wouldn't be easy, because she'd be leaving behind the familiar and moving into the unknown. Her son and daughter-in-law have been encouraging her to move for more than a year. She's talking it over with them and is beginning to work out the details. "There will be a period of adjustment," she says, "but I realize that moving closer would allow me to live more blissfully."

Living with your own brand of flair might not fit the image your grown children have of you. Helen and Ray wrote separate lists and, in comparing them, decided to sell their family home. "Over our children's objections," they explained. "We're renting a houseboat on Lake Union. We're newlyweds again, the grandkids like it—and our son and daughter are getting used to the new us."

Living with flair doesn't have to be a huge transformation; it can simply mean including the comforts that make your day special. It's a window garden brimming with herbs, it's tea in the afternoon with your sweetheart, it's setting the table with silver and china for two— just a grandchild and you.

It's taking care of your health and feeling your best. It's going to the park with your grandkids and swinging. It's planting a garden with them, weeding, and showing off the new shoots. It's serving lemonade on the porch and raking the leaves so the grandkids can roll around in them. It's wearing socks to bed and sleeping with the window wide open. It's clapping the loudest at your grandchild's piano recital.

Enlarge Your Grandparenting Circle

A close-knit nuclear family is very special, but a family made up of both related and nonrelated folks is also wonderful. Families can come from the same bloodline or they can be like a patchwork quilt—not always with the same background or pattern, but when they're gathered together they serve the purpose well. These days, families can be made up, more or less, of your children, your children's children, a half-dozen friends, an aunt and uncle, three distant cousins, a few neighbors, and a few stray pets.

A wise man once said, "You can love the whole world," and I think it's true; but even if you don't want to stretch that far, enlarging your grandparenting influence beyond your immediate family will go a long way toward making you whole. The more people you love and the more people who love you, the better. We all want to make a contribution, and when we reach out to just one more child, one more parent, we've started a ripple of kindness with far-reaching effects.

Children everywhere long for responsible, compassionate, caring adults who will give them attention, believe in them, watch over them, and help them up when they fall. Children need grandparents who are willing to work tirelessly and love unconditionally, grandparents who understand that love is the healing force that mends broken hearts and keeps families intact. A grandparent's love is the glue that keeps a family strong in troubled times and makes life sparkle when times are good. The younger generation needs and wants you to be actively involved in loving and guiding them.

Jane doesn't have any grandchildren yet, but she is a stand-in granny to her four-year-old grandnephew, Cole, whose own grandparents live out of town. "With him, I'm able to appreciate what I was too busy to enjoy with my own children. Like letting him hold his own popcorn and teaching him how to use a pay phone."

Besides being involved with his own two grandchildren, Grandpa Sam is a volunteer with Foster Grandparents. Twice a week, he spends the morning at a day care center, reading and talking to the kids who don't get enough adult attention. Arnie volunteers at a summer camp for kids with cancer. He has been doing this since his daughter died twenty-three years ago of leukemia. Grandparents make up a large percentage of the volunteer force in our country, which proves that whenever you do something for a another human being, young or old, whether related to you or a complete stranger, you get back as much or more than you've given.

Do something for others. Get out of the house. Join in. Don't indulge in martyrdom or the "poor me" syndrome. Your kids are involved in life's whirlwind as you once were. Now you have to grab hold of your pioneer spirit and bring good things into your life. If it's kids you want, look around you and get active where the young folks are. The world needs you!

Do Something Active

Chances are you will live to be eighty years old or more. If you want to stay young of body, mind, and soul while advancing in years, you've got to stay limber and keep moving. You've got to keep walking, thinking, and feeling. You've got to be active! It isn't age that makes you old; it's shutting down and withdrawing.

Most older people do not become bedridden. Recent research has debunked the myth of the inevitability of mental deterioration and senility as we age. You may not retrieve information as quickly as you once did (Who cares if you can't remember names and phone numbers from thirty years ago?), but your ability to learn stays the same, especially when you keep exercising your brain muscle. If your memory isn't as quick as your grandchild's, don't worry—you've got a lot more information stored than they do. You can keep each other on your toes!

Being around young kids will keep you young. Perhaps because to keep up with them you've got to be able to move; and to be able to talk with them you have stay up-to-date on the latest toys, styles, slang, and technology. In some ways, the young are your personal fitness trainers.

Staying active doesn't mean taking an hour-long walk and then lying dormant for next twenty-three. Being active is a style of life that starts with getting up in the morning, eager to get going, and ends with a refreshing night's sleep.

Just because you're at retirement age doesn't mean you should stop working, nor should you stop working just because you've retired. At sixty-three, Doris is making a killing in real estate. She begins her day in the gym and works with clients into the afternoon. In the evenings, she sees friends, attends lectures, movies, and plays, and has even been known to dance the night away. She's active in political causes and lobbies for saving the wetlands. She upholds the value of work, saying, "Work is a wonderful thing—it keeps me happy. I get depressed if I'm not involved and making a contribution." Helen Gurley Brown, the editor-in-chief of *Cosmopolitan* magazine for more than thirty years, says, "Work is my drug of choice." At seventy-five, she is taking on the overseas operations of the magazine and writing her fifth book.

My friend Carol, grandmother of two and docent at the Seattle Art Museum, started her own business giving high-class art tours when her husband retired. After working for so many years, he likes relaxing with no schedule, but after raising children and being at home, she likes being out and about.

Whatever you choose, make this your motto: *I take life easy, but I haven't slowed down*. After all, premature boredom is definitely worse than premature graying.

Reach Out to Friends

There's an old proverb that says *Take pleasure in your grandchildren, find solace in your friendships.* This suggests that it's a good idea to find meaning and fulfillment in more ways than through your little "love bugs." It's difficult because you've put your whole self—all your energies, money, and work—into your family. You wanted it that way and you're glad you did it. You will always be there for them and they know it. You adore them. They need you, yet sometimes you feel as though you need them more. And once in a while, it seems as though they are too busy to notice how much. The feelings come and go more easily when shared with a close friend.

You need friends to talk things over with, friends for fun and socializing. Friends are a source of comfort and strength when your grandchildren haven't called you in a month and you're missing them. You're willing to do most of the reaching out, but once in a while you'd like them to at least check on you now and then. Instead of making them feel guilty, tell a close friend how you're feeling; she'll understand—she's felt the same. Make a pact that you will call each other before you do something crazy like cutting a grandchild out of your will.

Statistics show that women will spend a portion of their life grandparenting alone, either because of divorce or death. Many men will, too. If you've already established a close circle of friends who meet your social needs, you're doing great. But if you're wondering what to do on Saturday night, you need to recruit more cronies.

You can start by putting more effort into your old friendships. Call up someone you haven't seen for a while. Just because your friend is part of a couple doesn't mean you can't include her. Invite the neighbors for a potluck or join a hula dancing group at the senior center.

Sunday at 4 P.M. is soup day at Alice's. Old friends and family are always welcome, and she usually invites someone new—her hairdresser, a neighbor, or the clerk at the post office. "Drop in any Sunday; bring bread, wine, or a sweet," her printed invitation says. It's an informal tradition that has been growing for years.

Make it your policy to have friends of all ages—and introduce your grandchildren to them. If you include the grandchildren in your social circle, before you know it they're grown up and stopping by to see you and catch up on all the gossip in your set.

Polish Your Grandparenting Style

"I don't want to be one of those grandparents who is known only for their gifts. I don't want to relate to my grandson just through material things," says Patricia. "I want to share my view of humanity, let him see how magnificently the world works. Together we'll see birds fly, flowers open up; we'll notice the seasons of the year. I'm going to take him to the beach and plant a small garden just for him. I want to introduce him to the arts by taking him to see *The Nutcracker,* and when he's four or so I'm going to take him to the opera. And I'll take him cross-country skiing so he can see the deer peeking through the bushes. I want to share the universe and see it through his eyes."

Before you were a parent and had children of your own, you probably imagined what it would be like to be a mother or father. You may have had a vision of yourself caring for a baby, and you were eager for your new role. You thought about it, dreamed about it, and made plans for the future. But it's slightly different when you become a grandparent, because in many ways it's easier to imagine yourself as a parent than as a grandparent. That is because, for most of us, aging is not a completely comforting thought, and we associate grandparenting with growing old. So even though you're excited about sharing in the life of a child again, you are aware that your life is going by faster than you planned. The grandparents I spoke with, however, reassured me that since grandparenting is one of the benefits of growing older, you might want to think about your grandparenting style.

No one prepares you for the position or even asks if you want it—you're appointed with no choice in the matter. You'll be expected to know what to do. You have to blaze your own trail and wing it. You have no control over when your kids have kids, but you do have control over how you behave toward them.

You can still make use of your best parenting skills, but unless you're caring for your grandchildren full-time, you will need to acquire some grandparenting skills to use in conjunction.

There is no one right way to grandparent. Grandparents can be feisty or sedate, unconventional or refined. What is your approach? After you've thought about your style, you'll have a basis on which to make your grandparenting decisions.

Establish Your Own Guidelines in Your Home

Ogden Nash may have said, "When grandparents enter the door, discipline flies out the window," but I'm not sure that's true. Kids often behave better with grandparents. Maybe it's a "company manners" phenomenon.

"When it comes to discipline, most of the time I'm a hands-off grandma," said Suzanne Priscilla Jane (she likes to be called by her complete name). "Except last year, when I decided to give my son, Kevin, and my daughter-in-law, Nicky, a day off. It started on Christmas Eve, when Jordan, my adorable six-year-old grandson, was all wound up. His behavior was wearing thin, and I didn't want the same hubbub to ruin our Christmas morning. So I announced to Kevin and Nicky that I was giving them a day off. Since we'd all been spending the day at my house, I'd be in charge and they could sit back and enjoy. At first I think they might have been insulted. I'd never interfered like this before, so perhaps they felt that I was implying they couldn't handle their child. It wasn't that; it was just that I wanted to make sure we all had wonderful day. I couldn't enjoy it with a six year old running the show. When they arrived the next day, I took Jordan aside and quietly told him the rules: 'It's Christmas,' I said, 'and everyone is going to have a wonderful time.' We had a private chat and I told him what was expected. Well, he was as good as gold and more calm than when his folks are in charge. Aunt Karen taught him to layer the potatoes and cheese in the casserole, and Aunt Kathy let him help make the chocolate silk pies. He was in his glory and perfectly behaved. It was a fabulous day."

Jordan learned that the way Grandma does things is different from his parents, and he respects her ways. Suzanne Priscilla Jane said, "My son and daughter-in-law even noticed the difference and thanked me for their day of rest."

Learning that there are different rules in different houses is part of growing up. Codes of conduct at Grandma A's may be stricter than at Grandma B's, and Grandma probably does things differently than Grandpa. Grandparents might do some things exactly like parents; other rules might be different. When Alex visits Grandma's, he knows that everyone takes their shoes off at the front door and that no jumping on the beds is allowed.

You can be loving and friendly and still establish your guidelines. It is an experience of discovery for your grandchild and a learning experience for you, too.

Enthusiastically Embrace Your Role

Although Janet's granddaughter Kate is eight years old, Janet refuses to get rid of the pink tricycle with the white basket parked in front of her condo door. The day I visited, there was a note to the UPS man, instructing him to leave the package in the basket. "The manager wanted me to get rid of her trike, but I refused," smiled Janet, obviously tickled pink by her rebellion. "I live for my grandchildren and don't understand these people who say; 'I raised my kids, now leave me alone.'" Janet, who is called "Bubbie" by her two grandchildren and dozens of surrogates, wouldn't think of going more than a week without a visit with her grandchildren. "I don't feel good if I don't see them. I've waited for them all my life." Indeed, she has. When her son announced that he was getting married, right away she was buying white baby outfits.

"But your son's not married yet," her friends objected.

"No, but he's engaged," she pointed out.

"To be a good Bubbie," she says, "you have to carry shopping bags with things—not gifts, honey, but things, like chicken soup. I'm a Bubbie, not a nanny, and I make chicken soup for everyone." She carries Jacob's and Kate's pictures for good luck and buys presents whenever it strikes her fancy. "It isn't gifts that spoil grandchildren," she advises. "It's letting them get away with stuff.

"Honey, when you get to be my age, there's not much left. Kids make you feel young. If you don't believe me, just take a bunch of youngsters to a nursing home and look at the old people brighten up. They keep you moving, honey. I look young and I act young, because I live for these two kids. They are the smartest kids, and I'm not just saying that because we're related."

Shaking her finger in the air, she warns, "People are missing the boat. Your grandchildren are part of you; you had something to do with creating them, so don't abandon them. Grandchildren give you unconditional love, and when you're old you need that love to keep going."

Janet points to a black-and-white picture of a woman on the wall of her den and says with conviction, "This is my Bubbie, who loved me from the day I was born, and that is what every child needs. This world would be a much better place if everyone had a Bubbie."

I see what she means.

Connection

Grandchildren are God's helpmates
in charge of softening our hearts
and opening our eyes and ears
to the simple sights and sounds
that bring us joy.

Grandparents are in charge of gentle
loving and forgiveness, for persevering
and strengthening the heart connection
in your family.

Become the Emperor of Attention

When I told Joyce I was writing a book about grandparenting, she said, "There's only one way, honey—be there for them." She's right. Being available and giving your attention is the greatest demonstration of your love.

Attention is one of the most important nutrients for any child's physical, emotional, and spiritual growth. Seeds don't grow into buds without tender attention, and buds won't blossom unless you carefully tend them: watering, feeding, keeping the bugs away, patiently overseeing. Children, like flowers in a garden, need countless hours of attentive care. A child who is ignored and neglected will wither, but with loving attention he will grow and thrive.

Research has found that you can put two of the same plants in the same soil and give them the same nourishment, yet the plant that gets a little chit-chat, a sign of caring and concern, grows faster and fuller. In just a few weeks, it exhibits luxurious growth, whereas the neglected one is scrawny and withering away. For children to thrive, they too need a daily dose of food, water, sunshine, loving care, and one-on-one conversation.

The attentions of grandparents are vitamins for a child's spirit. She may be able to survive without them, but essential ingredients will be lacking. This is your role: to now be the Emperor or Empress of Attention. You are the bestower of precious validation of the essence of your grandchild's soul. Because you've learned through your own experience, you can more easily recognize, sometimes better than parents, when and what kind of attention is needed.

You can give attention, even if you live far way, through phone calls, letters, and little treats that say to your grandchild: *You matter to me.*

You must walk a fine line between caring and meddling, however, so be sure to balance your attention with common sense. When the grandkids are with you, away from their parents, you can pour it on in any amount or form that you wish; but when their parents are there, the more subtle kind of attention is often best so as not to undermine the parents' efforts. As Paula advises: "When the parents are around, I let them set the tone, but I'm always paying attention to where and how I'm needed, and if I'm not sure, I ask."

There's a mighty reward in giving attention to your grandchild whether he or she is an infant, an adolescent, or an adult. Even if they don't thank you in words, you see it in the flowering of their being. As they grow and become who they are meant to be—more capable, creative, honest, kind, successful, and full of life—that's the reward for your labor.

Forgive It All

Forgiveness is the cornerstone of family relationships that endure. As well as ruining family harmony, long-standing grudges are damaging to the soul. They ensnare the innocent in their insidious web and slowly erode the essence of the entire family connection, often leaving the children among the casualties in their wake. We can always find reasons for justifying our anger—he did this, she did that—but litanies of how you've been wronged won't clear the air, ease the tension, or repair the damage. Only forgiveness can do that. To build strong ties with our loved ones, we have to recognize and accept their fallibility as well as our own.

We've all been wronged, mistreated, and misunderstood, but going over it *ad nauseum* won't heal the wounds. Blaming and pointing the finger only makes things worse. Holding on to anger is exhausting. And where are the children during all this conflict? Usually in the thick of it.

There's an edge when Martha and her daughter Kate are in the same room. As Martha fixes dinner, putting dressing on the salad, Kate opens the refrigerator door and pulls out the lettuce.

"What's the matter?" Martha asks accusingly. "Don't you like my salad?"

"I don't want dressing," Kate snaps.

Sitting at the table, the two grandkids can feel the tension in the air. They roll their eyes; they stare at the floor. On the way home, Kate says, "She always does that."

After they're gone, Martha calls her other daughter and says, "Kate made a scene again."

Wounds from the past, like boils festering under the surface, continue to infect the present. To go forward takes courage, because it requires that you reflect on the ways you might have contributed to the eruption. Take the risk of saying, "I'd like to understand why you're angry with me." Only when you see the part you've played are you ready to forgive. Begin by talking it through with a friend or yelling it out in the shower; cry about it, cuss about it, scream if you must—then forgive.

Forgiveness allows you to begin anew. It's a decision that allows the hurt to heal, restoring trust on the way. Forgiving does not necessarily mean forgetting, nor does it enable you to turn back the clock; but it does allow you to go forward. To forgive you have to see something other than the betrayal, other than the hurt. See the growth in the other person; see what else there is to see—the benefits to the children, for example. For what better reason could there be to choose to release the anger and move beyond the rift? Instead of defining a relationship by its strife and anger, forgiveness allows you to put it in perspective.

Weighed down by grudges, we don't have our full energy available for loving. When you are tense and withdrawn in anger, children tend to view that as a personal rejection. They are quick to blame themselves for the problems among the adults in their lives. Our job is to protect them, not break them down. We forgive, not out of weakness, but out of strength.

Refine the Knack of Friendly Conversation

Someone once said that there's nothing wrong with the younger generation that the older generation didn't outgrow. You might remember as a child hearing your grandparents asking, "What's the younger generation coming to?" Now you find yourself asking the same question.

Boys with earrings, girls with tattoos—these are phenomena you don't comprehend, and you're not sure you want to.

While their parents are freaking out about your grandkids' behavior, you are free to remain nonjudgmental, which is more conducive to dialogue than making threats and flying off the handle, as parents are prone to do. Your stake in your grandchildren is different from their parents'. You have a broader perspective. You see the whole picture. As a consequence, you can engage preteens and teens in a friendly conversation on difficult issues or problems.

Having a friendly conversation means that *you* do the listening while *they* do the talking. To get the ball rolling, use the following conversation starters (they will come in handy not only when you're talking with the grandkids, but also with their parents): What happened? How did you feel? What are you going to do? Is there anything else you might do? Is there anything I can do? The key to these questions is to be lighthearted when asking them. Whether it's a small upset or a big crisis, sometimes you're the only one who can think clearly.

While they were visiting their son, John and Carla's sixteen-year-old grandson Greg stayed out two hours past his curfew. Relieved that Greg wasn't hurt, yet frustrated that he hadn't called home, his parents were cross-examining him and yelling. "Don't you know any better?" his dad demanded. "How could you? You're grounded for six months."

"We were so worried," his mom cried. Greg shrugged his shoulders and went to bed without saying much.

John waited until the next morning when everyone had calmed down and privately asked in his quiet, grandfatherly manner, "What happened, Greg?" Over a cup of coffee, he asked his daughter-in-law, "How are you feeling this morning?" And while doing the breakfast dishes with his son, John asked, "I wonder if there is another way to handle this matter . . ." Through his calm questioning and listening, peace was restored, and Greg revealed that he had come upon a car accident and stayed to help the victims.

Whether it is your grandchildren or their parents who are upset, it's always advisable to wait until everyone has calmed down before you step in. You don't need to solve the problem, but by asking the right questions and listening nonjudgmentally, you'll help them find their own solutions.

Create a Grandchildren's Corner

When I was looking over the plethora of grandparenting books at bookstores, I was amazed to see how many of them were full of suggestions for activities that grandparents could do with their grandchildren. Every activity imaginable seemed listed somewhere: painting, knitting, quilting, candle making, basket weaving, coin collecting, paper making, butterfly collecting—the lists were endless. Do grandparents really need lists to know how to entertain and enjoy their grandkids?

It's true that kids need things to do when visiting. Expecting them to sit still is unrealistic, bordering on cruel and unusual punishment! Whether your grandchild is a roly-poly bundle of energy or a teenager bebopping to the latest music, he needs something to keep him occupied. If you do some advance preparations, you won't be tearing out your hair, thinking of ways to distract them from your valuables. (If you have things that you don't want curious toddlers to touch, put them away.)

Besides getting to see you, one of the pleasures of Grandma's house is getting to look at her stuff. "I always look in Grandma's and Pappy's basement drawers," Derek told me. Each time, he seems to find new treasures, comic books, tools, and car parts. One of his best discoveries was the inside of a golf ball. His grandmother has been known to leave special certificates hiding in drawers: *Good for one movie with Grandma and the friend of your choice.*

The stuff hidden in your drawers, basements, and attics is always worth a peek. My grandma had a button box that intrigued me for years. Kids love old-fashioned stuff—like typewriters and record players. Fill a treasure chest with nostalgic goodies. Old jewelry, hats, and gloves are good for many afternoons of make-believe.

Courtney, age seventeen, says, "I remember when I visited my grandma; her house transformed into a giant kitchen, blanket fort, playhouse, restaurant—just about anything I could get my hands into she let me look at."

When my daughter, Amanda, visited her grandma as a child, she loved to hide in the closet in the upstairs bedroom that Grandma Dorothy kept for all the grandchildren. At her other grandmother's house, she liked to peek in the closet and dress in the old clothes and shoes that Grandma kept in a basket especially for her. After she was dressed, she'd top off her outfit with a hat and high heels and put on a one-girl parade. When Stephanie was twelve, her grandma let her look through piles of scrap material, which prompted her interest in sewing, and together they made a lap quilt.

Create a grandchildren's corner somewhere in your house. Keep crayons, coloring books, paper, paste, stickers, and tape handy. Kids like to draw and paint at a very young age. Each year, ask them to draw a picture of you. Date each picture, frame it, or put it in an album; in ten or more years, you'll have a portrait history of yourself!

Just-for-kids spaces include boxes, closets, blanket forts, or cozy corners. Serve lunch in one and you'll have an instant party and a friend for life.

Write Them Love Letters

Letter writing is a beautiful way to give your grandchildren an inside view of you, themselves, and their family. Phone calls are handy for keeping up with your grandchildren's activities and fresh gossip, but the telephone is not as conducive to sharing secrets, family history, and matters of the heart. For that, you'll need love letters.

Love letters should always be written on nice stationery. For young kids, you can find brightly colored paper with kites and balloons. As they get older, choose something lively in a color you think they'd like. Each year, choose something out of the ordinary—sophisticated linen one year and parchment the next. Make sure to buy matching envelopes, stickers, or sealing wax. If you have an artistic leaning, write with a calligraphy pen. If you use a computer, choose a script font. You can change the color of the ink and style each year. Always sign your letter by hand. Fifty years from now, your grandchildren will be glad to have a sample of your handwriting.

Write your love letter at the same time each year, perhaps on their birthday or your birthday. Create an atmosphere that sets the tone for your letter: Light candles and put on music to set the mood; tune out distractions. Your letter is a reflection of you on this day. If you want it lively, put on upbeat music; if it's a letter of forgiveness, play a soft instrumental piece.

If you're not accustomed to writing down your feelings, you might have to practice and do drafts to find the words to match what you'd like to share. Love letters can straighten out misunderstandings and clear up unfinished business—so long as you write them without blame or guilt. If you're unsure about what you've written, read it out loud to a trusted friend for feedback.

Letters are also a wonderful means for documenting your family history. Usually, children know very little about your life as it was before they were a part of it. Share recollections from the past—yours and your family's. Your sisters and brothers and parents are your grandchildren's great-aunts and -uncles and great-grandparents—and the children should know their names and where they came from. You can enclose old photographs with the people and places identified on the back. Often, when older relatives pass on, priceless treasures of family history die with them, their boxes of old letters and photographs meaningless to their descendants. Give your grandchildren the gift of documenting their heritage for them.

When you write your letters, do it without expectation of a response. It takes courage to be vulnerable in this way, but the heart connection that comes from it is your reward. If your grandchildren do write, always respond with a genuine thank-you.

Before you send the letter, make a copy of the original on a similar piece of stationery. Store it in the plastic sleeves of a ring binder along with the letters they write to you. It's likely that your grandkids won't hold on to the letters—they're not at the sentimental stage yet—so you may decide to present them once again as a completed book when they reach adulthood. What a great one-of-a-kind gift!

Honor Their Confidences

Grandkids generally like it when you brag about them, but they hate it when you talk about them in the third person, as if they weren't in the room. There is a big difference between saying "We're so proud of you" and "You won't believe what Tommy did." Kids also don't like it when you share their private thoughts and feelings behind their backs. It makes them feel inconsequential, like you're ganging up on them. "When Grandma talks to my mom about me and I'm standing right there, I feel like walking out of the room," Susie told me. "The way Grandma talks about me makes me feel like I'm her pet and I don't like it."

If you want to tell about something that happened, ask the child's permission first. You might say something like, "Tommy, may I tell your mom what you said about the kittens, or should we keep it to ourselves?" This gives Tommy a choice in the matter, which makes him feel respected. By allowing your grandchild a voice and, whenever possible, a choice in the matters that affect him, you help build his self-esteem and teach him responsibility for his behavior.

If you want your grandchildren to talk freely about themselves, you have to respect their privacy and keep the conversations confidential. This is a challenge—after all, you love telling everyone how smart and clever your grandchildren are! This is natural; but before you start retelling your grandchildren's personal experiences, pay close attention to how they feel about it. Sharing every little thing that happens embarrasses them. More important, they won't feel they can trust you. If your grandson said something brilliant and you can't keep it as a private moment, at least don't repeat it in front of him. A fun idea might be to write down what he said in a journal. Keep it as your little secret until he's older. Then one day when he's visiting, bring out the journal and reminisce with him. You can both relive the moment then and have a good laugh together.

Grandkids need grandparents for many reasons, including as a trusted confidante. Someday when they're troubled, they might need a sympathetic ear and some honest advice. Lindsey, for example, has a closer relationship with her grandmother than with her mother. From a young age, she always talked things over with her grandma. "We're on the same wavelength," says Lindsey, twenty-seven. "My mom is very conservative, but my grandma is a free spirit like me."

If your grandchildren know that they can trust you because you've been trustworthy over the years, they will be more inclined to turn to you when they are in need.

Close the Generation Gap

Chloe has twelve grandchildren and was present when her youngest grandchild, Ilea, was born. "Being with my daughter Colleen while she was in labor was an incredible experience in itself. While I longed to protect her from pain, I knew I must not let maternal feelings overshadow the moment. I needed to be a woman supporting another woman who was giving birth." In relating to her daughter in this new way—woman to woman rather than mother to daughter—Chloe bridged the generation gap. And, along with a new granddaughter, a deeper dimension to their relationship was born.

A gap exists between the generations if you view each other only within the roles you've assumed. If your son sees you only as a mother, for example, and doesn't relate to you as a person, there will be an ever-widening gap between you, as his need for a mother decreases as he grows older. If you see your daughter only as your little girl, you will still be mothering her even when she's sixty and you're eighty. When you bridge the generation gap, you relate to the whole person rather than to a one-dimensional role. Through appreciating your similarities, respecting your differences, and understanding your common human struggles, you're able to enjoy one another more and grow yet closer as both of you evolve over the years.

Chloe has four adult children—three daughters and one son. She explains their relationship this way: "Being their mother is only one aspect of our relationship now that they are adults. My maternal lioness protection instinct emerges now and then, and I do worry about them even though they are all grown up. But I don't tell them what to do and I try not to give unwanted advice, because I haven't a clue how they should run their lives.

My daughters and I are equal women. I'm still their mother, but they also mother me when I need it. We're able to move back and forth in what we do for each other. They're grown women and we share in a grown-up way. We talk about women things—children, bills, sex, husbands, frustrations, feelings, hopes, and dreams. Cay told me that more and more she hears my words coming out of her mouth when she is dealing with her daughters. My son and daughters do a lot of the same things with their kids that I did with them—the good and the bad!

They've watched me grow up, too. I was very young when I had them and, after their dad and I divorced, I went through my "teen" period as they had done, and our roles were reversed for a while. We're there for each other; we're good friends."

Roles are like hats: You wear them at different times for different occasions. By taking off your parental hat, you're updating your image and letting them see your many facets.

Delight in Every Child

"I don't lump my grandchildren all together," says Marie. "I look on them like this: I have this grandchild, and this one, and this one, and this one, and this one. They're separate little people, not a bunch."

Whether you have two grandchildren or ten, each one is a distinct individual with unique talents, each a separate soul with his or her own destiny. Getting to know them personally is more rewarding than relating to them as a group. As you appreciate each one individually, your relationships will expand and bring you more and more enjoyment and delight. By spending one-on-one time with each of your grandchildren, you'll come to recognize the differences in their temperaments, dispositions, and personalities.

In order to know your grandchildren as individuals, avoid making comparisons. Billy may have walked by eleven months, but that doesn't mean Bobby will. And just because four-year-old Susie can read doesn't mean her four-year-old cousin should, too. Children grow and learn at their own pace, eventually getting the hang of what they need to know.

Take care to give attention to all your grandchildren. Giving your attention equally doesn't mean that you treat them all the same; because they are different, you should treat them differently. What it does mean, however, is that you don't slight one by preferring another. "Granddad likes my sister best," is a tragic statement to hear, whether it is accurate or not. Be sure to tell them, "You are my one and only Molly. There is no one quite like you; you're my one-of-a-kind girl."

Marie told me that when she went to see the family for the first time after the birth of her fifth grandchild, she was very careful not to look at the baby immediately. She greeted and hugged the older children first, because she didn't want them to feel less important. "I focused on the older ones until they wanted to show me their new baby. When they said, 'Nana, look at our baby,' I knew that they were ready. I didn't want them to feel pushed aside when I met my new grandchild."

Each new grandchild increases your capacity for caring. Your circle of love is expanding. New babies are precious, but so are two year olds. Older ones enrich your life in many ways, too. Eight and ten year olds are good companions for the afternoon, and teenagers make brilliant observations. Such a lovely bouquet—*vive la différence!*

Accentuate the Positive

I asked a group of kids ranging in ages from eight to eighteen what they liked about their grandparents. Here are some of the answers:

"Grandparents know only the 'good you,' and I like that. My folks see the bad things I do. But since my grandparents only see the good me, I'm nicer when I'm with them. I think they bring out the best in me."

"I know that they are always thinking about me—even though we don't see each other very often. They send me letters and little things in the mail. It makes me feel good to know my grandparents are thinking of me."

"It seems like grandparents think about you more than your parents do."

"When Nanna buys me things, she's happy. But when my mom buys me things, she isn't. I still let my mom buy me things, but it is more fun when Nanna does."

"I like going to Grandma Mary's house, because she is more messy than Grandma Hannah. Grandma Hannah is always wiping her forehead and says, 'Oh, me,' but Grandma Mary doesn't care if I spill something. She says the best thing about spills is that you can always clean them up."

"My grandpa is my favorite. He's dead now, but when I was with my grandpa, his friends would come by and they would always say,

'Your grandpa told me how good you're doing,' and it made me feel so good that he was always bragging about me. Since I didn't have a dad, my grandpa was always protecting me. I was my grandpa's little girl. He was proud of everything I did. If he were still alive, he'd be the first one I'd tell that I got accepted to college. I'd tell him all that kind of stuff. I miss him."

"Grandparents spoil their grandkids, but it's not the bad kind of spoiling—it's sorta like love."

"When you go over to see them, they are always nice, they don't yell, and they don't get mad. They give you candy and money. I like them a lot. I miss them and they miss me."

"One grandpa likes to go out a lot, and one grandpa likes to stay in, but they both like me."

"My mom doesn't like my grandma, but I do."

"I just like 'em."

By these answers, you can tell that kids understand what's going on behind the scenes. They know what's important and what you're doing for them. You are a comfort to your grandchild when you accentuate the positive in them. Accentuate the love and kindness and, even when you're separated, they'll have warm, fuzzy feelings and speak well of you.

Tell Your Life Story in Stages

Fran, a widow, said, "When my four-year-old grandson asked me, 'Grams, why didn't you get married?' I knew I needed to tell my story and I'd better start soon."

Telling your life story is important. It gives your grandkids a sense of tradition and belonging, allowing them to see how they fit into the family picture, and unites you in your common heritage. You can tell a personal vignette at any moment—standing in line, driving in the car, walking to the park, or gathered around the dinner table on Thanksgiving. Passing on your stories enriches their lives and lets them get to know you as a fascinating person who has lead a long and interesting life, beyond your role as grandparent. Kids are fascinated to hear that you didn't have TV and video games and shopping malls when you were a child; and they are equally delighted to hear that you played with dolls, built forts, had a baseball team, or helped your mom with your younger siblings—just like they do.

A life story told at just the right moment can teach and guide, comfort and soothe, heal and uplift. You've got a half-century of stories to tell, so you've no choice but to tell them in stages. Life stories give a sense of tradition and belonging. Age-appropriate stories are best—something the children can relate to. A six-year-old isn't interested in how you met Grandpa, but tell him about your first bicycle or how it cost you only a nickel to go to the movies and you'll have his rapt attention. Save the courtship stories for the teen years.

Through telling stories, you become a role model simply by sharing your blunders and your ingenuity in solving a particular problem. "You can learn a lot if you're lucky enough to get in trouble when you're young—like the time I took my dad's truck without asking . . ." So Grandpa Joe began his tale of borrowing the truck to drive into town and getting hopelessly lost, ending up two hundred miles from home before he figured it out.

Tell about your growing-up years and the most important people in your life. What do you know about *your* grandparents? Describe the characters of your story in detail. What did *your* grandma look like? "She had white hair, which she never cut, and she wore it in two buns on the side. And she always wore a blue-and-white stripped apron and smelled of honeysuckle."

Tell a story about a mistake or a bad decision you made. You don't have to supply a moral, because then you'll sound like a preacher and they'll soon close their ears. Kids are very smart about getting the point. Tell about a lie you told, the fish you caught, the concert where you saw Elvis. Becoming a skillful storyteller prevents you from becoming the rambling, absentminded type who repeats the same old line: "Did I tell you about the time . . . ?"

You're a walking history book; you've lived through "the good old days." Give your grandchildren a colorful peek into the past and a deeper connection to you.

Share Photo Albums
and Cookbooks

When Margie, a twin and a grandmother of twins, was a youngster, she loved to visit her grandparents' homes and browse through boxes of old photos. Enthralled by the pictures of near and distant relations, she coaxed her grandparents to tell the details of her relatives' lives. Eventually, she learned more about her family than her mother and father ever knew. Uncle Webster on her great-grandfather's side was a polygamist who had at least two wives that they knew of. A second cousin once removed was ordained as a minister through a mail-order course, and he traveled the country performing weddings and funerals. Eventually, he settled in a small town and established a pet cemetery. As a college student, Margie researched his life and wrote a freelance article about him which earned her a few hundred dollars. Searching through old photos and getting her grandparents to divulge the family skeletons sparked her interest in photography and gossip. It was, she is convinced, the springboard to her career as a photojournalist.

Seeing where they come from is entertaining to kids of all ages. Every family has secrets—a few skeletons in the closet—that are worth passing on. Remember that shameful secrets kept hidden eventually turn into lies, and then no one knows the truth. So what if Aunt Addie smoked a pipe, or Cousin Claude wouldn't get a job? You make it possible for your grandchildren to embrace their individuality when you reveal the eccentricities of their ancestors. Show your grandkids their mom's or dad's baby pictures; it enables them to see their parents in a whole new light.

Kids can also learn about their heritage through the family's favorite foods. It seems that every family has specific dishes they like to eat on special occasions. "No one makes spaghetti sauce with clams like my grandma," says Tony. "We always have prime rib and twice-baked potatoes on Thanksgiving, because no one in our family likes turkey," Mark told me.

Start when your grandkids are young by teaching them to cook some of your simple favorites, such as cinnamon toast and hot chocolate with old-fashioned whipped cream. Collect your favorite recipes and put them in an album, along with a story or reminiscence, and give it as a present. When Angela got married, her great-grandmother gave her the old family cookbook, stained and full of Grandma's scribbling in the margins.

Many of us regret not finding out about our ancestors from our grandparents. Even if your grandchildren don't seem too interested right now, they will someday treasure such heirlooms.

Deal With Divorce by Opening Your Heart Wider

Anabelle and Charlie have been married fifty-two years and have two sons, one daughter, and seven grandchildren. They also have three daughters-in-law, two sons-in-law, and six step-grandchildren. This is not the family picture they had anticipated, and their family ties are now more complicated than they ever imagined.

One out of two marriages in the United States ends in divorce. Divorce affects not only the couple and the children involved, it also affects you, the grandparents. Difficult and sad though divorce is, it could happen—or it may already have happened—in your family. To deal with it most effectively, you may have to learn to rise above your own discomfort and open your heart wider. For the sake of your grandkids, you might have to make room in your family for more step-grandkids, more in-laws, and more shirt-tale relatives than you ever dreamed of. You may have to maneuver your way through the mountains of anger, hurt, misunderstanding, confusion, insecurity, and jealousy that accompany divorce. Although you may disapprove of what's going on— and no one says you have to like it—you must set the tone and be a healing presence amid the chaos for the sake of your grandchildren. You can be the stabilizer, the safety net.

Kelly and Clark said, "We loved our daughter-in-law and were heartbroken when our son told us they were divorcing. It took us a year or so just to adjust to them living separately. Then suddenly they both remarried, and we inherited new grandkids. It has taken a lot of work on our part, but we have maintained a good relationship with all of the adults and can see our grandkids as much as we want."

If you find yourself faced with a similar situation, the wisest course of action is to stay neutral, listen more, keep your opinions to yourself, and open your heart wider. You have plenty of love for everyone. Your grandchildren are still your grandchildren, even if they don't live with your son or daughter full-time. They are innocent bystanders in the breakup, and you don't need to add to the fuss by divorcing them too. Maintain the family continuity by telling the children that you'll always be their grandparents and put your words into action. Keep your promises—call, write, invite them over, go to visit—even if it means staying at a motel down the road from your former daughter-in-law. Don't take sides or talk disparagingly about either parent; don't probe or pry for information. Be available and consistent in your love. Your grandchildren will be counting on your words and watching your actions.

As Kelly and Clark's family circle enlarged, so did their family events. Now when they host a gathering, it starts at noon and continues into the evening. Kelly schedules who comes when so that no one has to run into someone if they don't want to. It's a lot of extra work but, Kelly says, "We want to see *all* the kids, so I do whatever I can to make it smooth and enjoyable for everyone. We didn't expect our family be such a conglomeration, but we discovered we have enough love for everyone."

Love Your Son-in-law or Daughter-in-law

Maintaining a close relationship with your own children is natural, but establishing relationships with their spouses might seem awkward at first. You want to get along with your son-in-law or daughter-in-law, and to do that you must make a concerted effort and give him or her the benefit of the doubt. Abbey said, "I liked her because my son liked her. If my son is happy, I can be happy. But we had to learn each other's ways."

They will have different habits and opinions, so you must try to appreciate what they have brought to your family. You don't have to think, feel, or act alike to enjoy each other. What qualities do you appreciate in your son- or daughter-in-law? How have they enriched your life and that of your adult child?

If you want to have a relaxed and comfortable relationship, you must keep the lines of communication open. To do that you must respect his or her ways of doing things. You and your son- or daughter-in-law have many similarities—after all, you love some of the same people! And of course you have differences, but those differences don't have to keep you at a distance. If your daughter-in-law senses that you value her outlook and are willing to hear her point of view, she will, in return, be open to hearing from you.

Christine says, "After my grandbaby was born, I'd call to check on her and even when my son-in-law answered the phone, I'd ask for my daughter. One day she was out and since I was eager to know about the baby's progress, I talked with my son-in-law instead—and he gave me all the details. From then on I made it a point to talk with him not only about the baby, but about *his* life as well. Our friendship has really grown."

Make room in your conversations for your son- or daughter-in-law too. Ask your son's wife about her day or how her work is going. Listen to her answers before you respond or jump too quickly back to the subject of your grandchildren—they don't have be the topic of conversation *all* the time. Invite your daughter-in-law for an outing and pay for the baby-sitter. Ask your son-in-law to lunch and tell him that you appreciate how much he cares for his family.

The wise parent strives to get to know the children-in-law early and, instead of insisting that things be "my way," makes every effort to handle differences constructively—by accepting the differences rather than resisting them. Remember that you are setting an example for everyone. A family that values all of its members equally is a nurturing environment for children.

Leave the Disciplining to Parents

A well-deserved benefit of grandparenting is that you don't have to be a rule maker or enforcer. By now you probably have the skill to use your authority without being authoritarian. You can use the more subtle approach, such as, "We're not going to do that now," and the distraction technique of "Look at this."

I don't advise reprimanding the grandkids in front of the parents. Clear away the things you don't want the toddler to touch, and if the parents are around, tell them what's bugging you and ask them to handle it. If it's okay with them that you take charge, proceed with caution just the same. This is a sensitive area, so apply your best diplomacy and tact.

Three-year-old Nicholas was jumping up and down while riding in the car. Grandpa sternly told Nicholas to sit down. Nicholas obeyed, tears running down his face. Amy, the daughter-in-law, whispered to her husband loud enough for everyone to hear, "He wasn't bothering anything." The fight was on.

As a grandparent, finesse is required. Scolding is out and artfulness is in. When Tommy is hitting his brother and no one is stepping in, you can intervene without punishing. Distraction with a splash of humor usually gets things moving on the right track more quickly than other techniques. Instead of threatening Tommy or sending him to his room, you can say something like, "I don't like fighting; let's play a game," which will surely get his and everyone else's attention. When Annie is having a temper tantrum because she wants more ice cream, you can smile kindly and say something like, "I'm like you—I can never get enough ice cream. But it's not good to have too much."

Without disciplining their actions per se, you can set limits simply by letting everyone know what behavior is acceptable to you: "You can eat in the family room, but not in the living room." "You can play in the attic, but these are my boxes, so don't bother them." If you don't agree with how the parents are handling the situation and you think they want your input, talk to them privately, but don't take disciplining your grandchildren upon yourself.

Parents are the ones in charge of teaching daily living skills; you are in charge of patience, kindness, and good-natured understanding. This is your time to be compassionate and easy-going, and no one has to get their feathers ruffled.

Collaborate and Work Together

Raising a child is a joint venture between two generations—the grand generation (that's you) and the middle generation (that's the parents). Learning and working together to find the best, most fruitful ways of doing things for the good of the upcoming generation is more productive than struggling on your own. Each generation has a worthwhile contribution to make.

Here's what I mean: Remember the story of Suzanne Priscilla Jane on Christmas morning? Well, there's more to the story. Dinner was on the table and the family of eleven were standing at their places, ready to sit down. Suzanne asked the family to hold hands and close their eyes as Julie sang the blessing. As she was about to begin the Lord's Prayer, six-year-old Jordan started laughing. Suzanne opened her eyes and gave Jordan "the look," and immediately he bowed his head and was quiet. But Suzanne's son Kevin and daughter Konnie burst out laughing.

"What's going on?" Suzanne asked.

"That look," Kevin said.

"We recognize it," chimed in Konnie. "You gave us that look when we were young—and it still works."

Old tactics are tried-and-true, and the middle generation can still learn from you.

The front walk was covered with pinecones. "If you pick them up, Jordan, I'll pay you a penny for each one," Suzanne said. Jordan did a thorough job and Grandma had to pay up. Three hundred pinecones equaled three dollars. "I thought that was a bit too much money for a six-year-old, but I had promised, so I kept my word." The next time Jordan came for a visit, there were more pinecones on the walk and naturally he wanted to get paid for picking them up. *What should I do?* Suzanne wondered. *After all, fair is fair.*

Kevin spoke up and told Jordan, "No, Grandma is not going to pay you this time. This time you do it to help out. Sometimes we do things for money and sometimes we do things to be helpful."

"I understood what he was saying," Suzanne said later, "so I let Jordan help me and I thanked him."

It's both fun and exciting to be a member of a family that honors and appreciates your way of doing things. Families work best when everyone feels competent and valued. Whatever problem you may be facing, you'll find the most creative solutions when you seek input from each other. If one member doesn't know the answer, you can figure it out together. Raising a child is a joint collaboration. And remember, your every little facial expression, every tiny gesture, every action, is sending a message to all the generations around you.

Give Mementos

As we baby boomers become grandparents, we're spending money on our grandkids. Whether you are buying the first teddy bear or paying college tuition, remember that it isn't gifts that spoil children—it's trying to buy love through material things. So long as you're not stingy with your love, you can give as many gifts as you can reasonably afford. Since we all know that we can't take it with us, we might as well enjoy watching our loved ones reap the benefits now.

Jean says, "Gifts are one way to stay connected when your grandchild is far away. There's joy in deciding what to give; looking at all the wonderful toys, books, and clothes adds to your sense of connection to your sweet one. You're doing something with only them in mind." It doesn't have to be a new or expensive gift; it can be a something you made or had stuffed in a drawer.

While I was away at college, my grandmother, who was very poor, used to send me care packages full of my favorite homemade graham cracker sandwiches. Opening the box comforted me when I was homesick, and it felt good to know that she was thinking about me. She told me she was praying for me, and I believed that her prayers kept me safe. I didn't have the heart to tell her that by the time the crackers arrived they were smashed to bits, but it didn't matter; it was the thought and the prayers that counted.

Family mementos mean a lot. Margaret and John passed on to their young grandchildren the very picture books that they had once read to their own small children. As the grandkids grew and showed an interest in grown-up books, they passed those on, too. The grandkids, now adults themselves, vividly remember these gifts; they were in fact more meaningful than receiving something new. Kids do like the latest fads in toys, but they also appreciate the sense of connection that an heirloom holds. My brother inherited a pencil collection, and when he looks at it he remembers the little house where he spent his childhood. Abram gave his five-year-old great-granddaughter, Alisha, a flashlight from his tool box, and she slept with it for five months straight. Marvin gave his father's pocket watch to his grandson, who will someday pass it on to *his* son.

At about the age of six, kids enjoy collections. Help them start one and add to it each year. Each birthday or at Christmas, pass down a piece of china, silver, or crystal. Give a piece of your jewelry or pass down a tool. Enclose a card with the history of the memento.

A wise woman once said, "A grandchild knows your worth; you don't have to prove it, but you can still bring packages."

Avoid Getting Caught in the Middle

"My family is like *Family Feud* and *Days of Our Lives* all rolled up into one," a fourteen-year-old client told me. "My mom's mom and my dad don't speak to each other, so my mom is refusing to go to my dad's family reunion this summer. My mom will be mad at me if I go with my dad, and my dad will be mad at me if I don't."

As preposterous as this may sound, it was only the tip of the iceberg. By the time my young client came for counseling, she was depressed, not eating, skipping school, and having suicidal thoughts. She was caught in the middle of a terrible family feud with nowhere to turn. Her grandmother did not like her father from the day her parents were married, and the battle had been waging for more than sixteen years. My client was the innocent victim of quarreling, name calling, finger pointing, and blaming.

If you want to offer a safe harbor for your grandchildren, you must avoid getting caught up in family feuds. To do this, you must put the needs of the children above everything else. You must rise above your wants and desires and make the highest choice on behalf of your grandchild. Ask yourself, *If this child were me, how would I want to be treated? What is the best choice for the good of my grandchild?* You might not like the situation, you might think your son-in-law is goofy, you might wish her parents would go away, but for the sake of the grandchildren, you must do what's right.

To see how you are doing, ask yourself the following questions: *Do I side with one parent or the other? Do I blame the other parent? Have I talked badly about one of the parents in front of the child? Do I talk badly about the in-laws in front of the child or with either parent?* If you answered yes to any of these questions, you're in danger of getting caught in the middle.

The maze of family issues is tricky terrain: Who is going to spend the birthdays with whom; in whose church will the kids be raised; do we spend the holidays with her parents or his parents . . . It's slippery business, and you have to watch your tongue. Telling your daughter-in-law, "Your mom is a selfish witch" is no way to improve relationships—even if your daughter-in-law has said that very thing herself on numerous occasions.

Never make assumptions. Ask for clarification for what you don't understand. Memorize this line: *Let me think that over and get back to you.* Be flexible in how and when you celebrate important dates. Just because you've opened presents every Christmas Eve for the past thirty-five years doesn't mean you can't do it on another day. Remember that it's the feeling of warmth and being together that matters, not that you do it the exact same way year after year. Be willing to make the generous offer, to go the extra mile. Don't insist on having your way. Uncompromising stalemates in a family are not conducive to loving relationships.

Follow Instinct and Etiquette

If you want to avoid your adult children singing the "I can't send her home—she's my mother" blues, don't wear out your welcome by staying for a month when you were invited for a week. And don't take over running the show unless you've been asked. When you are invited for a visit, ask for clarification: "Would you like it if we stayed part of the time in a hotel, so you can have a privacy break?"

Even if you're sincerely trying to help, resist the urge to take over, especially with first-time parents. First-timers need to practice; if you constantly take charge, they'll feel inadequate and won't like you coming around. Guard against falling into the role of "responsible parent," telling your grown children how things should be done. Be sure that they are seeking suggestions before you give advice. Sensitivity to what the grandchild's parents would like from you can smooth the way and facilitate future visits. There will be clues as to what is appreciated and what isn't. Pay attention!

You need to remember that you are their guest. If they ask for input, great; but realize that this is their shining moment for demonstrating how they've accepted their adult roles and responsibilities. You can all share in the appreciation of the children. After all, there's absolutely no one else with whom they can gush so openly about the marvelous accomplishments and charms of their offspring!

Stay in the background and offer specific help: "Would it be helpful if I made the beds?" Use your instincts. Some parents appreciate your noticing what needs to be done and pitching in without asking; others want you to offer before jumping in. Tell them: "I'd like to help in any way I can, but I don't want to interfere, so please let me know what you'd like."

You can have a wonderful visit, lightening their load without invading their privacy, by using manners and guest etiquette. Don't reorganize the kitchen cupboards unless asked. "Honey, are there any chores you'd like me to do?" is better than jumping to clean the oven. "Would you like me to get up with they baby?" is better than racing down the hall at midnight, assuming that you're being helpful.

Remember that your adult children are new to the parenting role and they want to be viewed as competent. If you show confidence and trust that they can make the decisions now, you can prevent a stressful relationship from ever developing.

Rise Above the Small Stuff

When my first book, *Wonderful Ways to Love a Child,* was published several years ago, I received hundreds of letters not only from parents who found my book useful, but from grandparents who found it inspiring. Here's an excerpt from a letter written by a woman in Ohio:

> My daughter is going to have my first grandchild in two months. When I was at the bookstore today, I saw your book and started skimming through it to see if I wanted to buy it for her. Reading it was very painful, and there were pages that made me cry, but I couldn't put it down. I won't go into the reasons, but the truth is I was not a very good mother. I wish I would have known about the little kindnesses and the common sense you write about so that I could have done things differently. I am trying to make amends with my daughter, and I want to be a much better grandma. I just pray for another chance and that it isn't too late.

I received similar letters from parents throughout the United States and Canada who recognize their mistakes and want to do better now that they are grandparents. I also heard from grandparents who were estranged from their adult children and their grandchildren, carrying the baggage of hurts and misunderstandings for so many years that they couldn't remember what started the feuds. One women wrote, "I have no idea why my son is still mad. We haven't spoken for six years and now he's having a child. What do I do?" I wrote back: Rise above the small stuff, ask for forgiveness, and make amends.

Touched by these letters, I was encouraged, because by owning up to their shortcomings, these grandparents had already made the first step toward improving family relations. Whether it's with your own child or with your grandchild, so long as you're willing to forgive the small stuff and do whatever it takes, it's never too late to have a wonderfully satisfying, uplifting relationship. It is never to late to build a bridge and cross the rift.

Anything standing in the way of a loving relationship with a grandchild—including a feud with his parents—is small stuff. You can rise above it by first acknowledging what you've done to contribute to the mess. Apologize by saying something like, "Yes, you're right. I wasn't listening." Then ask for forgiveness, make amends, and behave as kindly as you can. If they have complaints, listen to them with an open mind. Respond with something like, "I see what you mean," "Help me understand," or "I'll think that over."

When you rise above the small stuff, you're setting a good example for everyone in the family—and that's good for you and your grandkids.

Courage

A grandchild knows your worth;
you don't have to prove it. If you
feel useless, don't be concerned,
your uselessness is needed. You are
like a huge tree with great foliage.
And the folks who are engaged in
useful activities will need sometimes
to rest in your shade.

Allow Them to Come and Go

Jean has firsthand experience in allowing her adult kids and grandkids the freedom to live their own lives. But it's not always easy. Her oldest son, Craig, is a pilot in the air force; he and his wife, Christine, live all over the world, wherever his tour of duty takes them. Her son Todd, with wife, Reija, and baby, Emma, is working and studying abroad. Jean wrote to me on the day they left for Germany:

> Today I'm in mourning. I vacuum the empty room so I can drown out the sound of my crying. A small stone in the corner, a cup under the bed. Remainders left—like me. Two bath toys sit on the patio table; baby cereal in the cupboard. I slip my hands into his worn shoes. When did my little boy become this distant man—so far away? Last night I found a washcloth with Emma's sweet scent on it. I placed it under my pillow for comfort. Going through old school papers, clippings, I found a poem Reija wrote. A poem to the man upstairs. A man with a piano: "A Mother's Lament." How intriguing Reija is. So hard to read, but so much to know. I love this little family—so beautiful—why so far away?

When your children are growing up, you tell them to drink their juice, eat their vegetables, and don't go out without a coat, because that's the healthy thing to do. Leaving the nest is the healthy, natural thing to do, too. To reach their full potential, they need to follow their own dreams, make their own decisions, and experience the outcomes. Interfering with that—by letting them know how needy you are or that you want them to come back home—will undoubtedly have a negative effect on their personal growth as well as on your relationship.

That kind of pressure puts unreasonable demands, as well as guilt, on your children, no matter how much they love you. Giving them space does not mean that you must deny how important they are and how much you love them. But it does give them room to grow and make their own way in the world. When you're with them, let them know how special that family time is for you. Show them how much you like hearing about what they're doing and support them in that. But make it clear that you respect their independent lives.

As Jean says, "After the initial separation, I had the 'lonesome grandma' blues; now I'm accepting—I have no other options."

Whether your children and grandchildren live down the road or on the other side of the country, whether you see them once a week or once a year, they are building a life separate from you. That's the way it's meant to be. You can sob on your friend's shoulder every now and then about how much you miss them and wish that you could witness every new thing your grandchildren do. But if you want to have a mutually satisfying relationship with them, you must let them come and go easily.

Indulge Yourself to Your Heart's Content

Isn't it delectable to play hide-and-seek and pretend you can't see the little darlings hiding under the kitchen table? Isn't it glorious to hear the squeals of delight when you pretend you don't recognize them in their Halloween costumes? Didn't you enjoy buying her that sweater her mother liked but couldn't afford? Isn't it spectacular to see her wear a tiny pink tutu and perform in her first recital? And doesn't it just take your breath away when he invites, "Grandpa, let's play catch!"? Playing with grandchildren is fun at its absolute best.

The greatest reward of grandparenting is that you can have fun with your grandchildren and no one will object. You can indulge them to their heart's content. And, more important, you can indulge them to *your* heart's content. You can take them to the zoo, the circus, the movies, or the mall. Take them to the park to play; you can sit and watch them or you can join in. You don't have to follow anyone else's guidelines or worry about what other folks think—you're allowed to invent your own "grandparenting rules."

You can let them splash in the bathtub and sleep on the floor. If you want to and you can stay awake, it's okay with me if you let them stay up past *your* bedtime! You're the grandparent and at this stage in life, *you* are supposed to have fun. You have a significant role and a substantial job to do. When your grandchildren are with you, it's your moral obligation to teach them the important things: how to whistle and snap your fingers, how to bake brownies and lick the spoon, how to plant snapdragons and chase the slugs. Give them a brush and a bucket of paint and teach them to paint rainbows. Show them how to toast sunflower seeds and how to peel a pomegranate. If you don't do it, who will?

When your grandkids are teenagers (regardless of what you might have heard), they're still eager to learn from you. It's your responsibility to introduce them to life's survival skills, like how to play a mean game of Scrabble and how to keep a poker face when holding a full house. When that's done, be sure take them to a Chinese restaurant and show them how to eat with chopsticks (if *you* don't know how, they'll gladly show you!). Let them wash your car; if you hand over the keys, they'll gladly run your errands or be your chauffeur. Go to one of those photo booths, cram in together, and have your pictures taken. Take your granddaughter to high tea at a fancy hotel; invite your grandson to monster truck races. Or do the reverse! Ask your grandteens to take you on a tour of a music store and teach you the words to their favorite songs. Feed them lunch at a sidewalk cafe and recite the words to *your* favorite song.

Whether fun is plain or elaborate, free or extravagant, the beauty of grandparenthood is that you can indulge without guilt. As seven-year-old Adam observed, "When Grandma's bossing me, I get more done and have more fun." That's all the permission you need to carry on in any way you wish.

Put Parenting on the Back Burner

It's a relief to be a grandparent instead of the chief cook and bottle washer. You no longer have to build character, take control, or dish out the discipline. You're indispensable, but you're no longer running the show. You are still somebody's parent and always will be, but now you do whatever parenting is needed in a relaxed, lighthearted way.

Even though they're adults with kids of their own, your children still need you. I asked Craig, twenty-eight, what he still wanted from his parents, and this is his answer: "Of course love and support, but also a base to keep coming back to when things happen that make me feel I'm not on the right course. I remember the values and ideals that I was given while I was growing up, and as an adult I realize how much they shape my life and the decisions I make. Now I ask opinions from my parents instead of avoiding them as I did as a teenager. I seriously consider their views. I also ask about specific things too, such as finances, purchases, and investments."

Todd called from Germany in the middle of the day to ask Jean in Arizona how to cook chimichangas. "That was not a question I had prepared myself to receive from him," said Jean. Todd had gotten a job as a Tex-Mex chef and he didn't know how to cook! The next time, when Todd called about baby Emma's injured hand, Jean wrote in her journal, "I guess he still needs me a little—that's nice."

According to Pam, who says she had a love/hate relationship with her own daughter throughout growing up, "The best part of parenting is grandparenting. Now that my daughter is a mother, things are better between us. I don't have to improve on her anymore. She's given me the most beautiful grandchildren, and I'm glad we are no longer fighting."

Fred agrees and says, "My grandchildren bring my son and me together by separating us. Now we focus on the children instead of on each other. We keep a respectful distance."

Grandparent is a better part to play than parent. You can take pleasure in your grandchildren like you never could in your own children. Free from the heady responsibilities and daily stress of parenting, you can be more loving, patient, generous, and easygoing. You can be fun to be with. Now that your children are parents, they understand you better and no longer blame or denounce you for the real or imagined injustices they suffered at your hands. The grandparenting years are a time of reconciliation between your children and you. With a grandchild in your life, you can forget all about being parental; you can become your best, most loving, delightful self.

Treat Them Tenderly

Leslie, a single mother of two, went to live with her dad, Bob, after her mother died. They both agree that it's an arrangement "of the most extraordinary kind."

"Watching my dad with his grandchildren has blown me away," Leslie told me. "He's a different man than the one I grew up with. I was afraid of him because he was strict and intense. But with my kids he's easygoing. He respects me and he shows it."

Bob admits, "I use to tell Leslie, 'Don't do that—do this.' It's natural for a father. But I don't do that anymore. I'm here when she needs me."

Tenderness is very important for children, and grandparents are good people to give it. It's often hard for parents to show tenderness on a day-to-day basis. Remember what it was like to be the head of the family, running a household? When you're a parent, you're the chairman of the board—and you're also the secretary, treasurer, and janitor, not to mention cafeteria manager and groundskeeper. As a grandparent, however, you're no longer in the rat race—you have the luxury of retirement; because you're not in charge of making sure they do their homework, eat their vegetables, and get to bed on time, you can slow down, read a bedtime story, and show a lot of tenderness.

Grandchildren bring out our tender sides. Maybe it's because we understand more of what life is all about. Maybe it's because the pace of our lives has slowed down enough to enable us to relax more than we could when we were young parents. Our children have their hands full raising our grandchildren. We understand, we can identify, and it humbles us.

James is six-feet-three-inches tall with hands so large he can hold his week-old granddaughter in one. "I'm mush," he laughs as he picks her up. "You're Grandpa's little angel." And as he coos, you can see the tenderness in his eyes.

There are many ways to show your tender side. Take Bob, for example. You might not describe him as tender, but he certainly was. He had a way of talking to his grandchildren that let them know how much he really cared. Whenever he went to visit them, after being in the house for only twenty minutes, he'd stand up, jingle the change in his pocket, walk to the window, and ask, "How's your car running?" which his teenage grandson, Brian, immediately understood to mean *How are you?*

Then Bob would ask, "Do you need new tires?" which, translated, meant *Is there anything I can do for you?*

"There *is* a funny sound when I start the engine," Brian might say, and they'd walk out together to give the car a once-over. Bob showed his love by being there and taking care of what he knew best.

Whether you're cuddling the young ones, wiping runny noses, bandaging a skinned knee, or cheering on the team, you've got a gentle sensitivity that grandkids need. The world can be harsh and cruel, and children have to deal with insensitivity and pushiness every day. There are plenty of people to knock them around and set them straight. It's no wonder they brighten up when they're with you.

Remember: It's Okay to Say No to Babysitting

You're surprised that you don't feel the urge to babysit. Perhaps you thought that the babysitting gene would activate as soon as the baby was here, but it didn't and you're not sure what to do. You've always been available for your children and you adore your grandchild, yet you don't want to babysit and you're feeling guilty. You wonder if something is wrong with you. What do you do? How do you say no?

If you don't like to babysit or if your schedule is too full to provide routine day-care—it's okay to say so. Successful grandparenting doesn't necessarily include regular babysitting; and even if you're willing to be available once in a while, consider it carefully before you sign up as the permanent sitter.

Marilyn and Hank retired from their first careers and are busily carving out a new life. Hank's building a studio in the back of the house, where he intends to sculpt and paint the mornings away. Marilyn works two days a week in retail, takes dancing lessons, is president of her garden club, and tutors adults in English. They adore their four grandchildren, but don't like babysitting except in a pinch. Laura, a single grandmother who works fifty-plus hours a week, loves to spend time with her new grandbaby, but can't commit to anything regular. Charlene and Dan like the grandchildren to visit, but they don't want to equip their house for child care—they'd rather go to their son's house where the stroller, high chair, crib, and toys are handy. Maureen, on the other hand, likes to babysit and has right to first refusal. Her daughter-in-law checks with her first before she calls a different sitter.

Whatever is true for you, by using the "two T's"—talking and timing—you can put together a workable alliance. Try these babysitting guidelines:

- *Talk babysitting wishes over in person and well in advance.* Don't wait until the last minute, when they need a sitter in an hour. It's better to talk in relaxed atmosphere so you can be clear about your wishes and hear their expectations. Then you can devise a plan with no hidden agendas and avoid hard feelings.

- *Let the parents know what you're willing to do.* They might be assuming they can count on you whenever they need to. Are you willing to babysit during the day, in the evenings, or on the weekends? What about overnight? Do you want to keep plans flexible or do you want a regular schedule? How much advance notice do you need? Should you be the first sitter they call? Would you prefer to be the backup?

If you're babysitting just because you can't say no, you'll start feeling resentful, and nothing ruins a relationship between you and your children faster than secret resentments. Living with a little guilt because you said no is far better than pretending you like babysitting when you don't.

Make Room for the Other Grandparents

If you're lucky enough to really like your darlings' other set of grandparents, you have nothing to worry about; but if you aren't sure you want to share your grandbaby, you're in for a jarring awakening. Like it or not, you've got next-of-kin! When a grandchild is born, *both* sets of grandparents want to be involved—and rightly so!—but until you get accustomed to each other, jealousy and suspicion could put a strain on your relationship.

For example, the other grandma might be afraid she'll be left out, and that fear may make her less friendly. Don't take it personally—just be aware that her fear is getting in the way. She'll be less threatened if you reach out. Send her a card congratulating her on becoming a grandmother. Invite the in-laws to your home for coffee and discuss your joint little bundle of joy. Be patient if it seems as though they're pushing you away; tell them you're glad that the baby has so many grandparents who love him.

Being a mature in-law requires a conscious effort on your part to make the experience pleasant; it's an ongoing process that doesn't have to be competitive. A bad relationship with the in-laws sours everything; you don't want an undertow of hostility affecting your family relations. And with a new baby in their lives, the last thing your children need are sparring parents!

You want your grandchildren to have full, rich lives, and having two sets of relatives is part of that. Just because the in-laws are spending time with the baby doesn't mean they are taking something away from you. You may be envious from time to time, but don't complain or act hurt. If you've raised more than one child, you've lived through sibling rivalry, and you probably told your children countless times, "I love you both." When you start battling for the grandchildren's attention, you're engaging in in-law rivalry and making matters worse.

Barbara said, "I don't feel any sense of competition with my in-laws over my grandbaby. Jake is her grandson, too, and as important as Jake is to me, I can relate to her as a grandmother." If people get possessive with those who are important to them, it can poison the relationship. Put your energies into delighting in the moments you have and be glad that your grandbaby is loved by others. "I don't begrudge the time Jake has with his other grandma," says Barbara. "I want everyone to love Jake."

Assume the best! You can always step in if things should get off track, but don't steer them that way by assuming the worst. This is not a contest. Your grandchildren will benefit from all the attention and love coming their way.

Quiet Your Critical Voice

Parents are the gatekeepers of your grandchildren, so if you want to spend time with the little ones, you obviously need to stay on good terms with the middle generation. One way to do this is to remember that most criticism is unnecessary and seldom useful. It pushes your loved ones away and creates resentment, anger, and hostility. The parents of your grandchildren *want* your approval. You show it by not criticizing how they're raising your grandchildren.

It's not helpful to your adult children to have their parenting skills analyzed and evaluated. They are learning as you did and they need practice. "Why are you picking up the baby every time she cries?" is not a useful question—it implies that Mom is inadequate. "You're spoiling the baby if you let him sleep with you" is not helpful either—it implies that you doubt their judgment. Interfering in how they raise their children benefits no one.

If you have an idea about how to get the kids to pick up their toys, for example, don't share it in the middle of the problem or in front of the kids. And before you say even one word, consider it carefully, making sure that your son or daughter is willing to hear your point of view.

Criticism and sarcasm have no place with your grandchildren either. Asking, "Why do you wear your hair that way?" or saying, "Baggy shirts make you look ridiculous" is belittling. A child who is constantly criticized starts condemning himself and doubts his own self-worth. And when you criticize your grandchildren, their parents take it personally.

If you've said something that your children or grandchildren took as criticism, you'll be able to tell by the tone of their voice or the fact that they don't say a word. Even if you didn't mean to criticize, apologize right away: "I'm sorry, I know I sounded critical. I didn't mean to."

Be pleasant, gentle, and loving in what you do and say. Except in cases of real neglect or emotional, physical, or sexual abuse, keep your opinions on childrearing to yourself. You'll be doing yourself, your children, and your grandchildren a favor. If, however, you are concerned about your grandchild's physical well-being, by all means do whatever it takes to make sure the child is safe. But be sure your grandchild is truly in danger before you interfere.

Smile and Laugh Together

It hasn't been scientifically proven, but I think it's true just the same: Grandparents smile at children more frequently than parents do. Everyone coos over babies, but by the time the baby is running, tracking mud into the house, and wiping dirty fingers on the freshly hung guest-bathroom towels, the parents have stopped smiling. It's not because they're mean, it's just that they're distracted by the dozens of things they have to get done. You, on the other hand, are smiling and laughing more. Your kids have moved out and your house stays tidy, just the way you like it. Dave, who inherited twelve grandchildren through marriage, explains it best: "I enjoy my grandchildren and I'm thankful I don't have to raise them."

Your facial expressions give your grandchildren information. Maybe the reason they run over to you and climb on your lap is because of your friendly-looking face. Tune in to your grandkids' sense of humor and you're in for a special treat.

At ten months old, Emma was already developing a sense of humor. Jean experienced it firsthand: "When we had dinner or whenever we had something to drink, I would take a sip of my drink and then say *'aah'* and look at Emma, because this would grab her attention and she'd give me a big smile. I did this for several days. One day, I came into the room where Reija was nursing Emma, and I could see Emma look up at me. With her eyes on me, she pulled away from her mom and with a big smile she said, *'Aah.'* She looked very pleased with herself. It was very pleasing to me too, because this was our private joke—it really tickled me."

Marie told me a story about her grandson's sense of humor. After Lavran, one-and-a-half years old, got his first haircut, he climbed on his grandfather's lap, patted Grandpa's bald spot, and said, "Grandpa got a big haircut." When he realized that he'd made everyone laugh, he felt good about his accomplishment. By cherishing your grandchild's first attempts at humor, you're letting him know that he's fun to be with.

Humor encourages teamwork. Pay attention to the tone of your voice and the manner with which you ask the kids for help. Obviously, "I need your hands to help wash the dishes" said with a friendly tone is much more effective than a stern, "Help with the dishes!"

Laughter is also a great way for kids to get over embarrassment. If your five-year-old granddaughter falls out of the swing, she'll be startled at first, wondering if you saw her. But if she rolls on the ground giggling, other kids will join in, and she'll forget her initial fall. When kids learn to take themselves less seriously, they learn to take setbacks in stride.

Grandkids are with you for such a short time. Take every opportunity to smile and laugh when you're together.

Bask in the Miracle of Birth

Your first grandchild had such an impact on you—like the first of anything—that you might not be sure how you'll react to the second. Bette has six grandchildren and says, "I've been astonished to see that each one comes into the world with his own personality, destiny, and soul. I could sense it. Only one hour old, physically helpless, but spiritually powerful."

Becoming a grandparent, whether for the first or fifth time, is a blessed event. Meeting your newborn grandbaby is deeply moving—instantly your heart melts. Regardless of how many times you've been through it, newborn grandbabies tug at your heart. In an instant, you're thanking God for the miracle and praying for hers, yours, her parents', cousins', aunts' and uncles', the in-laws', and the world's well-being. Your grandbaby has put you in the presence of the Divine; suddenly it feels as though you're standing on holy ground. It's breathtaking to see a tiny child so innocent, dependent, and vulnerable.

Art, a seasoned grandpa of three, says: "Being at the hospital when my daughter gives birth is a troubling experience. I don't know what to do with myself. I read the newspaper and pace the floor. I don't know how, but my being there seems to give moral support, so I'm glad to do it."

George, a fifty-year-old first-timer says, "Being a grandfather, or Papa, is a terrific feeling. As with our own kids, it is amazing to see the progress little Emma has made in just ten months. She's evolved from a totally dependent infant to a real being with personality, intelligence, emotion, love, and creativity. Her rapid growth in intellect just overwhelms me. She has learned so much and has found so many ways to capture the hearts and souls of those who know her. And, of course, she has us all wrapped around her little finger."

A close relationship with a grandbaby acquaints you with the depth of ordinary things—things you often overlook. With your grandbaby, you watch the human spirit unfold and are swept away.

"My feelings for Emma grow each time I see her, each time I hear her sweet voice on the phone," adds George. "She is a precious little girl, with a mind of her own and a strong will. She has all the love, warmth, and affection to set her on a course for success."

You can't help it—you're weak in the knees and ready to do amazing things on behalf of your grandbabies' welfare. You identify with other grandparents, and you've probably felt as George did when he said, "I'm thrilled and honored to be a grandfather. I only hope this world will be a kind and hospitable place for Emma and those who follow."

Get Silly

It's been said that the truly wise woman allows herself a little foolishness now and then. Hopefully, you're wise enough by now to know when and how much is needed. Let's face it: If you can't be playful with your grandchildren, you're well on your way to becoming cranky, somber, and downright disagreeable. You'll miss out on the best part of life, and no one will like being around you. If you tend toward seriousness, perfectionism, or self-criticism, you need to let your hair down and spend a day with the grandkids. As Courtney, seventeen, points out, "Grandchildren stir up the house and keep the atmosphere lively."

Invite your grandkids over and get silly. If you can't do it for yourself, do it for them, because experts in child development agree that kids who are lighthearted and playful are happier and have more friends. Think of it as teaching them people skills. Tell your grandkids jokes and riddles; sing and tap your foot. You'll be helping them develop their funny bones, which is bound to win them pals. See the humor in your situation, and your grandkids will learn to look for silver linings.

When you're listening to music, telling stories, reading books, and laughing, your time together will be relaxed and they'll want to come see you more often. Instead of complaining that they never come to visit, invite them over and teach them to do the jitterbug, the slide, or the twist. Ask them to show you *their* latest moves. If you can't relax with them because you don't want your house messed up, they won't stay long. But if you're willing to roll up the rug, they'll want to drop by just to see what you're up to.

Soon after Joe introduced his soon-to-be-teenage grandson to National Public Radio's *Car Talk,* they scheduled regular Saturday-morning dates to listen to the show, eat donuts, and laugh. Learn a few magic tricks to entertain them. They'll laugh for sure if Grandma learns to juggle! Laughter gets the endorphins flowing, which has a soothing effect on the body. The mind continues to grow when it's stimulated, and the body has tremendous power to rejuvenate when it's relaxed.

Zachary, age four, describes his granddaddy this way: "He's old and funny." That's certainly better than what Jessica said about her grandfather: "He's not funny." Developing your funny bone is well worth the effort.

Real maturity retains something of childhood, so make your grandparenting style upbeat, lighthearted, and fun. Doing silly things together builds trust. It will help the kids deal with their own anxieties and frustrations. So long as you aren't poking fun or teasing, it's a healthy, wonderful family atmosphere.

Seek Balance in Your Life

Holding the baby of your "grown-up baby" for the first time is a thrill. After all, there's a creative link between you. But holding the baby is just the beginning; there's much more ahead for both of you. That's because becoming a grandparent is not just about the baby—it's also about you.

Becoming a grandparent is a rite of passage like any other—accepting and welcoming another phase of life. If you approach this stage of life moaning and dragging your feet, you'll be missing a lot. Whether you're forty, fifty, sixty, seventy, or more, becoming a grandparent with all your heart and soul will bring you more satisfaction than holding back.

Just like getting married or having a baby is a big life event, so is becoming a grandparent. But unlike those other life-transforming events, grandparenting doesn't have to consume your every waking thought and action. That's what makes this time in life so special—you have time to devote to *you*.

We've all known grandparents who talk nonstop about their grandchildren; and though we appreciate the love they have for their little ones, we sense that something is missing. Their lives seem out of balance. We're saddened and we wonder why.

Life has many dimensions—why not explore them all? When you are with your grandchildren, be with them totally: Pour all your time, energy, thoughts, and actions into them. When you're away from them, devote your time, energy, thoughts, and actions to yourself, your spouse, your friends, work, and hobbies. You can develop yourself and become a balanced, fascinating person, or you can spend this time doing nothing and become flat and one-dimensional.

Carly, fifty-nine, is a juicy woman who took up photography after her husband died. The walls of her home are lined with photographs of family, flowers, animals, and sights from Puget Sound. On the weekends, she takes walking tours, taking pictures of things that bring her joy. "After my husband died, I held tight to my children and grandchildren; they were my salvation for a while. Eventually, I forced myself to try new things. It's not always easy, but I know it's good for me."

What does it mean to be a grandparent and live your life in balance? It means loving yourself too, not just living through your children and grandchildren. It also means reflecting on your skills and discovering talents that still can be developed. Perhaps as a teenager you had a musical interest which has been kept on the back burner your whole adult life. Take it up now! Enroll in a class, sign up for lessons, or join a choir. Donna is taking tap dancing. Jim is a wood carver, presenting his first show. Bill is developing his theatrical bent, clowning at holiday parades and children's hospitals. Take time for yourself each day, nurturing yourself, learning something new.

Grandparenting is part-time occupation with lots of bonuses, including the chance to live your life in balance.

Stay Close

If you want to spend a lot of time with your grandchildren, chances are your number one enemy is geographical separation. One study showed that if you live within five miles of your grandchildren, you'll have more than a hundred visits per year. On the other hand, if you're separated by more than a hundred miles, your visits will drop to three or four a year.

Like most grandparents, grandkids are on the move, too; they're involved in as many activities as you are, so don't lay guilt trips on them if they're not with you every minute after you flew five hundred miles to spend a week with them. As Karen, a grandma with a good sense of the ridiculous, said, "I was just glad they recognized me."

An important aspect of fostering close relationships is face-to-face visits, so if you live in another city, you'll have to go out of your way to make each visit memorable. In between visits, you'll have to keep the lines of communication open—to stay close and actively involved.

If you live at a distance, you've got to be willing to travel. If you have to fly to see them, take advantage of airfare wars and go as often as your budget (and your grown children) allow. Don't get stuck in the fear-of-flying rut, staying home because you're afraid to step on an airplane. If you're truly too fearful, invite your family to visit you—and pay for their tickets.

Grandma Gertie was a wealthy miser. Moaning that she hated to fly and whining that no one ever came to see her, she spent most of her days alone. When one of her teenage grandsons volunteered to visit during spring break if she'd "pop for a ticket," she mumbled an excuse that meant *I'm not parting with my money.* Her kids tried to talk sense into her, but she kept her money in the bank and stayed lonely. Don't let this happen to you. If you've got the money, treat yourself as often as they invite you, or ask point blank if you might visit next month. Don't let ideological, religious, or other differences keep you away. You don't have to believe that your daughter-in-law is the most wonderful woman in the world in order to enjoy your grandchildren (but remember to keep your opinions to yourself!).

After visiting, you're likely to feel lonely and miss your family even more. The ache is the deepest right after your visit, and it's sometimes hard to get back into the swing of things. It's natural to be weepy and a little depressed for a few days or a week. Allow yourself to feel the pain of missing them, shed your tears, and then reach out to a friend, preferably a grandparent who's in the same boat.

Stay in Touch: Send Mail, Make a Phone Call

Staying in touch with children and grandchildren when you're separated (not only by miles but by busy family schedules) is tricky indeed, but nevertheless well worth the effort. You can always pick up the phone, but sometimes grandkids are too busy or too young to talk. When they do come to the phone, frequently they're not very talkative or they have call waiting and you are put on hold.

Although it's always great to hear your loved ones' voices, there are other ways to keep in touch that are fun, too. One way is to start a routine of conversing through electronic mail. E-mail is here to stay, so if you haven't already tackled this 20th-century convenience, consider taking an adult-education course at a community college and start learning. You'll be thrilled by how easy it is to stay in touch with your grandchildren who would never before write you a note. Katherine says, "My contact with my nineteen-year-old granddaughter has increased 100 % since I got online." And your long-distance bills can be a thing of the past, as e-mail costs nothing more than a local phone call—even when corresponding halfway around the world.

Maybe you won't have the opportunity to see your out-of-towners over the summer and need a fresh way to stay connected. One of the easiest ways is to make a "story scrapbook" of some favorite family anecdotes. Carry a tape recorder around for a day or two and make an audiotape to send them. Tell them what you are doing as if they're by your side. Send your recording along with a blank tape for them to do the same and send back to you. You could try recording a video too!

I also like the idea of a friend of mine (who got the idea from a friend of hers) of increasing communication quarterly via a family newsletter. When Gerta's grandkids were young, she drew pictures for them and wrote with large marking pens so they were easy to read. She included age-appropriate stories and asked questions to encourage the kids to write back. As the kids got older, she wrote about her experiences in school. When her grandson took up soccer, she researched soccer history and passed along some sports trivia. When her granddaughter got her first job, Gerta wrote about *her* first day on the job; and when her grandson went to college, she reminisced about *her* days in a dorm. She even gave some disguised advice in the form of her favorite quotations and proverbs.

Newsletters are also a clever way to pass along your family history. You can copy pictures of your ancestors so everyone knows whom you are talking about. Encourage the grandkids to contribute to future editions. In her first edition, Gerta announced a contest to give her newsletter a name. The winner and six runners-up got a prize (she has seven grandchildren). Frequently, she bribes her clan with contests—everything from a day at the beach with Grandma to a shopping spree at the mall. And when she is questioned about her trickery, she doesn't bat an eye; she says, "It's a grandma's prerogative."

Give the Relationship Time to Develop

There is a thin line and a big difference between grandmothering and grand*smothering,* and you need to know the difference. Babies who have not seen you for a while will not be keen on your swooping them up or trying to coax them away from their parents. They'll need to get their bearings and check you out first. Don't be offended when they cling to "home-base" relatives; they'll warm up to you if you let them go at their own pace. Don't be hurt or put pressure on the mother to make the child come to you. If you can be patient and pleasant, the baby will eventually feel safe enough to venture over. When she gives you the signal by putting her arms out, you can hold her, but be sure to let her go right back Mommy or Daddy when she wants to. It's a getting-to-know-you game, so have fun with it. You can coo and cuddle to your heart's content, so long as you don't gobble her up.

It's the same with older kids. If they've been traveling on a plane or by car, they'll have a lot of pent-up energy when they arrive and may need to run around to work it off. They might want to eat something, use the bathroom, turn on the television, check things out. Again, don't feel hurt if they're not ready to sit down for a long heart-to-heart right away. The best visits are one-on-one; and if you let things evolve, you'll have plenty of chances to catch up.

Realize that a friendship with your grandchild does not happen instantly or automatically. Don't insist that he play his saxophone or that she do her ballet routine five minutes into the visit. Your goal is to get to know each other personally; like any relationship, that requires give-and-take. Children have their own rhythms, needs, and desires; if you respect that, they'll know it and want to be friends. If you push, push, push, you may get a hug or an answer to your question, but your relationship will remain superficial. If you want something deeper, you'll have to allow them control over the timing.

Obviously, each child is an individual—some are more cuddly than others, some are more verbally expressive. You can understand their needs by listening carefully and paying attention to body language. Don't tell *them* what *they* want, and if they pull back from you, back off. Don't let *your* needs get mixed in. Tracy told me, "My grandma instantly attached herself to my soul and my very existence. She stopped living for herself the moment I was born and she's still living for me today. I'm glad we live at a distance."

The key to a lasting friendship is to know and respect each grandchild as a unique individual and take the time to cultivate a real relationship.

Talk About the Difficult Things

"Gramee, why you crying?" Wanting to tell the truth but not wanting to scare seven-year-old Nicholas, she answered, "Because I'm sick and crying makes me feel better." Talking calmly about difficult and painful things with grandchildren is not as frightening as you might think. What is likely to scare them more than talking about what is happening is being left in the dark to imagine what's going on. Kids are able to talk about the realities of life—from birth and illness to God and death—so long as the adults deal with the issues calmly and openly and don't overload them with information or opinions.

Eighteen-year-old Kimberly and her seventy-nine-year-old grandmother, Alice, were having lunch and visiting one sunny afternoon. "Grandma, you've got sauce all over mouth—here's a napkin," said Kimberly.

"There, did I get it?" Alice asked.

"No, you've still got some on your chin," laughed Kimberly, who then teasingly asked, "Grandma, am I going to have to wipe your chin when you get old?"

"I hope not," answered Alice. "I'm not planning on being helpless, but you never know where life is taking you. Isn't life funny? You'll be old someday, too."

"Yup," answered Kimberly. "Life goes backward."

"God must have a funny sense of humor," Alice remarked.

"Everyone thinks God is so serious, but he must be looking down and laughing," said Kimberly.

If you're willing to talk about the hard stuff, the kids probably will be, too. And although these subjects are important, you don't have to approach them with a doom-and-gloom attitude. You can be matter-of-fact and positive even when you're facing difficult issues such as illness or death.

Everyone dies. If you don't acknowledge that once in a while, it will be quite a shock to a child when it happens. It's good to have a little practice talking about these things. You don't have to be formal about it; there are plenty of moments when the opportunity naturally arises, such as the death of a pet, or even in the context of a children's movie. Fairy tales are rife with loss and death and are good springboards for broaching the subject. It's okay to talk about death— not in a morbid way, but as a fact of life.

Perhaps a friend of yours has died, and your grandchildren are aware that you'll be attending the funeral. Perhaps a beloved relative is ill and not expected to live. These are appropriate situations for you to share your feelings and talk about the natural order of things. If you're grieving the loss of a friend or relative, don't hide your grief from your grandchildren. They should see that you love and are loved by many people, and that we sometimes lose people we care about. It's okay for them to see you cry. When you are suffering, it's okay to tell them so. The healing for you and your grandchildren comes as you share your feelings and talk openly about the person who has died.

Look Through the Eyes of Your Grandchild

"We went outside and there was a dandelion that had gone to seed," Rebecca, the grandmother of a two-year-old boy, remembers. "To me, it was a weed so common that I'd stopped noticing them long ago; but for my grandson Noah, it was a spectacular find. I showed him how to blow the seeds into the wind, and I could see by the look on his face that he was completely caught up in the excitement of this event. It blew me away to watch him with those dandelions. It taught me to look at the world through his eyes."

Imagine what it's like to be seeing, tasting, and hearing for the very first time. Everyday happenings become marvelous spectacles—birds singing, sun shining, tulips blooming, friends laughing. Look at the world through the eyes of your grandchildren, and you see things anew. You're enthusiastic and life is magical. An airplane flying overhead, a jogger and his dog passing by, a butterfly fluttering in the yard—all are captivating delights to a child. Kids are spontaneous—that's part of their charm. They don't bother with logic or rationality; they don't get hung up on being consistent. They're lively, inquisitive, and eager to explore. When you see through the eyes of your grandchild, your daily routine is once again filled with wonder. The world is friendlier and so are you.

Grandchildren give you hope and reassurance. Rita says, "They inspire my imagination and give me fresh ideas. When I'm stuck in my watercolor class, I imagine how one of them might paint the picture, and then I'm able to express what I was struggling with earlier."

These are the advantages inherent in grandparenting. Not only do you get the joy of watching your grandchild's face light up as he discovers that water is good for drinking *and* splashing, you also get another chance to splash if you want to. You can teach him how to click his tongue *and* you can click yours. You can read him *Mother Goose* and enjoy it too!

"Kids are honest," says Helen, the grandmother of five. "And it's such a relief to be told the truth. My seven-year-old granddaughter said to me after I told her I was going on a diet, 'That's good, Grandma, because you're not exactly fat, but you're not exactly skinny.'"

By looking through the eyes of your grandchild, you get double the blessings.

Always Be with Them in Spirit

A friend of mine owns a gift shop and told me about an elderly woman who purchases tea sets to give to each of her great-grandchildren. These are not your average, run-of-the-mill tea sets; they are the highest-quality china, hand painted, special-ordered from England. Each time a new great-grandchild is born, she orders a new tea service. There is nothing out of the ordinary about buying expensive presents for grandchildren—many grandparents do that. What makes this story stand out is how she intends to give them. She places each tea set in her attic, along with a note for the designated child. No one in her family knows about her plan—it is her secret. After she dies, when her family is sorting through her things, they will discover the special presents and notes that she has left.

My friend did not know any more of the particulars, but it started me thinking about what a legacy that will be. I wonder who this women is and why she has chosen tea sets. Are they a symbol of something meaningful in her life? Will her great-grandchildren understand the meaning of the tea set and why it was chosen as her last earthly gift? It's almost as though the gift is given from the other side. There's considerable forethought and planning in giving such a gift, much love and dedication in leaving the beautiful bequest. She must hold her great-grandchildren in her heart each and every day.

What will the children think and feel when they discover the tea sets? What has she written in the notes? Will the great-grandchildren use the tea sets? Will they pass them on someday to their own children? Think of the stories they will tell while serving tea. Surely they will feel her presence.

I can see a twinkle in her eye as she places each tea set in just the right corner of the attic. She has a sense of humor. She must know that death is an illusion, and perhaps it is through the gifts that she is saying, "I'm with you in spirit. If you doubt it, serve tea and think of me; you'll sense that I am very close by."

You don't have to wait until you're gone to be spiritually connected to your children, grandchildren, or great-grandchildren. You are always connected through prayer, meditation, and love. Tell all your grandchildren: "I'm always with you in spirit, loving you, and cheering you on."

Pray for your beloved ones and tell them that you are. Like Grandma Olsen always said, "I'm loving and praying as best I can."

It's reassuring to know that someone out there in the universe is pulling for you, rooting you on. Knowing that there is a special grandparent who loves you no matter how far away you are, how old you are, how wrong you are, is a boon for the soul. Knowing that if you ever needed them, they'd be there for you is a nice feeling late at night when the winds are howling outside your door.

Fight the Good Fight

Many grandparents are rightly concerned about the conditions in which children are growing up these days. We're troubled by the violence on the highways and the crime in our communities. We're concerned for their education, health, and economic future. Will there be money for it all? When they grow up, will there be enough jobs to go around? Will they be able to pay the rent, buy a little house? We're bewildered about what the future holds.

We're also concerned by the troubled children we hear and read about. We don't understand why or how they got to be so unhappy and hostile. It distresses us to think of aimless children, angry, hurt, and lost. We ask ourselves what happened. How does a trusting baby come to lash out in such negatives ways in so few years? Does anyone care? We ask so many questions, but we don't have the answers. We wonder if anything can be done and who will do it. We're perplexed by it all.

You've probably guessed by now that I'm an advocate of mature, unconditional love as the most powerful force in the universe. Coupled with that, however, I imagine that there are significant causes in which grandparents can be involved to get things rolling in a positive direction. For example, if a group of grandparents met regularly to do intensive research and problem solving on behalf of children, I think they could find some do-able solutions to these difficult problems. Perhaps you might organize a community think tank to address the social issues. A "Grand Think Tank" focusing on problems facing our youth and senior citizens could be a vigorous force for good. All it takes is a few committed people to make a change.

The needs of children and senior citizens are very similar. Professor David Fischer of Brandeis University has proposed an intriguing plan. Instead of supporting people with Social Security at the ends of their lives, he says, it would be cheaper and easier to give each American a financial grant at birth that would be invested over his or her lifetime; then, during the senior years, everyone would have a secure pension. Professor Fischer has worked it out and says that the initial investment would cost the public less than Social Security. I know that this isn't the answer to all our social ills, but brainstorming sessions, neighborhood forums, and national summits among the generations could awaken expertise now lying dormant and tap into a wellspring of sensible resolutions.

I suspect that the energy released and the ideas concocted by grandparents brainstorming on behalf of children would be noticed, especially if you distributed press releases, invited city council members, wrote letters to editors, circulated petitions, and called the local television and print media. You could hook up with church youth groups and children's social service organizations such as Girl Scouts, Boy Scouts, or 4-H. Make banners and organize a march; you could call it "Children and Grandparents in Action." Perhaps your church, synagogue, school, or YWCA might be willing to cosponsor your event. Who will be the chairperson? How about you?

Pass Along Sentimental Keepsakes

If you're reading this book, you're probably a grandparent and it's likely that your grandparents have already died. Although they are no longer with you in body, they're certainly with you in spirit, and chances are you have a few keepsakes—a brooch or pocket watch, a set of china, a quilt, some old letters, a family Bible—that evoke memories of them. Maybe you even have a few faded black-and-white photographs of them as children.

My grandmother had three fine oak pieces of furniture: a worn round pedestal table on which we ate many Sunday dinners of chicken and dumplings, an oversized rocking chair that swallowed me up when I sat in it, and a grandfather clock with a swinging pendulum. My brother, sister, and I have each inherited one piece, and when I eat at the table, rock in the chair, or hear the clock chime, I'm flooded with memories of my dear, old-fashioned grandma.

My grandma saved green stamps. Since she was blind, she couldn't see to paste them into the books, so she stored them in a small chest until one of her grandchildren could paste and organize each book for her. To me, at nine years old, it was a highlight of my week when Grandma asked me to help her paste the stamps, count the books, and look in the catalog to see what we could buy. I loved licking each tiny stamp. I felt so grown up and proud to be Grandma's guide as we'd walk to town to shop at the green stamp catalog store.

The taste of stamps, her iron bed, the flower garden, the feel of her hands touching my face to see what I looked like—all are permanently etched in my mind. Sweet memories of simple everyday pleasures—nothing fancy, yet so extraordinary. Memories so strong that when I tell my daughter about the great-grandmother she never met, she feels her presence, too. One day, I'll pass on Grandma's grandfather clock to her.

A keepsake is a treasure whose worth is found in your grandchild's heart. You may never know for sure what it means to him or her, but you can guess from the warm feelings you share. Whether you pass along a special piece of jewelry, a record collection, a tool box, or a worn flight jacket, you're giving a symbol of the eternal tie between you. And whether you pass it down now or after you're gone, you can be sure that for them its value increases with each passing year.

Share What You Know

Your granddaughter may be a whiz kid in calculus and your grandson a star second baseman, while you are puzzled by her computer and unable to swim as far as he can. But even though your grandkids seem to know more and can do more than you did at their age, you aren't all washed up yet. Theirs is a different world than the one you grew up in. And though their rock videos and Nintendo games may seem Greek to you, the skills you learned as a child may be equally foreign to them.

You've got plenty of useful and practical skills your grandchildren need, not to mention a great degree of discretion and common sense. Do your grandkids know how to plant a bulb, clean a fish, weave a daisy chain, or harvest a vegetable garden? Do they know that applesauce and gravy don't have to come out of a jar? My daughter, Amanda, for example, was amazed to learn that her grandma could get spots out of her favorite sweatshirt and hem a skirt so she could barely see the stitches. She loves it when Grandma comes to stay, because she'll learn a new survival skill that I haven't honed. And on top of sharing her skills, Grandma keeps freshly sliced fruit in the refrigerator, ready to eat, a luxury Amanda dreams about long after Grandma's gone home.

It's a funny sort of thing that, unlike parents, grandparents don't have to lecture or pontificate to pass on what they know. While showing your grandchild how to sew curtains, bake a pie, change a tire, or throw a pot, you can toss in your philosophy at the same time. You can give them a lesson in living, and they won't object. They love it when you talk to them.

When her three-year-old grandson, Riley, swore in front of her, Linda said, "We don't say 'God' unless we're praying." Riley must think it's a great rule, because Linda overheard him passing it on to his dad and his buddy. Be friendly and upbeat as you set down your guidelines, and they'll take it in: "At Grandma's house, we put our dishes in the sink first, *then* we watch videos."

"My grandpa can do things my dad won't do," began twelve-year-old Nick's term paper. "He showed me the difference between a steelhead and a lake-bound rainbow trout. He lets me use his hook sharpener after a snag. Grandpa says that testing the line and being patient are the keys to success when I'm fishing. Don't pull his head out of the water or he'll spit out the hook. Don't horse the fish in. Grandpa taught me how to read the water and get my hook to the bottom. When we go fishing, we have to dress right. I wear long johns, hip boots, and a jacket. He's won lots of trophies but he says obeying the rule of the outdoors is more important. Never cheat. It's not the size of the fish, it's the outdoors. That's my grandpa's rules for fishing. My grandpa is my teacher and I am happy when we are fishing."

You are a teacher, a guide, a mentor, a model for living. Your grandchildren may not do exactly what you say, but never doubt for a moment that they are listening to you, imitating you, emulating what you do and what you say. Even from a distance, they are observing you. What do you want them to know?

Hang Out in The Moment

Hanging out with a grandchild—tiring though it sometimes can be—is one of life's peak experiences. Parents are so absorbed with the chores and responsibilities of daily living that they hardly have time to read bedtime stories, let alone play checkers, blow bubbles, paint pictures, pick dandelions, and catch bugs. You, on the other hand, can take time to treat yourself and your grandchild to the simplest yet most rewarding pleasures: not doing much of anything. At this stage of your life, letting another year go by because you're "too busy" is not a smart idea. Postponing by saying "maybe another time" is depriving yourself of living.

Nana Marie and her two-year-old grandson, Lavran, spent half the day scouting for the perfect rock. It was to be his first Christmas gift to his momma. Walking around the garden, Lavran picked up dozens of rocks, discussing the merits of each. This one was too rough, that one was too small, this one is not the right color.

"Nope," he said, shaking his head as Nana showed him dozens more. Finally settling on "that *big* one," a smooth flat river rock, their choice was made. Straining to pick up the rock, Lavran said, "I can do it." But it was too heavy.

"Let's lift it together," Nana said. Bending over, Nana held up one side and Lavran the other as they placed the rock in the red wheelbarrow. Then slowly, step by step, resting now and then, they pulled it into the house for wrapping. First Lavran chose the orange tissue paper—and used half a roll of tape to fix it. Then he added a layer of pink tissue and used twenty more strips of tape. He loved that tape. They placed the rock in a box, and Nana tied it with a green ribbon. Lavran used more tape to stick the red bow and eight name tags to the package. Now it was ready to place under the tree.

"I can do it," Lavran said. So Grandma bent down, Lavran held up his end, and together they carried the gift once again. Lavran found the right spot under the tree.

On Christmas morning, Lavran's package to his mother was the first one opened. Everyone oohed and aahed, and Momma was so happy as she opened her son's first present to her. And it had been chosen, wrapped, taped, and given because of Nana's patience.

Hanging out in the moment is the gift you give to the both of you. It matters not what you do, but rather that you are together peacefully—serenely enjoying the rocks, the gentle breeze, an ice-cream soda, or a bedtime story. It's a gift that touches both your souls.

Remember That You Are Not Alone

Grandpa Charlie likes jigsaw puzzles and bargains and is always looking for both. He buys puzzles for less than a dollar at swap meets and garage sales. His wife, Grandma Mary, and their two granddaughters tease him because they can remember only a half-dozen times when he bought a puzzle that actually had all the pieces. But he doesn't care; he likes his hobby and taking his chances.

Each member of our family is like a piece in a jigsaw puzzle—part of the whole. If one part is missing, the picture is incomplete. No piece is more important than another. Like a puzzle piece, you have a part, you belong, you fit; and along with the others, you make up a whole.

You are important to your family, even if at times you feel deserted and alone. They cannot forget you, nor can you forget them. Once you have loved somebody—your mother, father, husband, wife, son, daughter, grandchild—that person will have a permanent place in your heart. Even if they have disappointed or mistreated you, you cannot get rid of them by wishing or willing them away. You cannot throw them out of your heart, even though you may try. You are part of your family, and they are part of you.

Be grateful to your family for all that they have taught you. They have been your teachers. You would not know what you know without them. You've shared ups and downs, good times and bad. Haven't you become wiser, more compassionate, and forgiving because of the people who have touched your life? Haven't you learned more about yourself? Are you not richer of spirit?

Blessings for ties that bind. Be grateful to your children, your grandchildren, and all who have touch your life. Don't take anything or anyone for granted. Make the effort to be thankful, to count the blessings that come with each and every family member. It is through gratitude that we become aware of the presence of God. God is working in your life. You are not alone. The whole of the universe is working together. We live on the earth; we breathe the same air. Be grateful and you will feel the connection.

When you are grateful, you will come to love yourself and all that you are. When you are grateful for where you've been and what you've done, you are at peace—with yourself and with your family. And that, my friend, is the perfect legacy, the very best gift you can give to the future generation.

Acknowledgments

I could not have written this book without my "grand consultants." Each with his or her own area of expertise, they bring such style, grace, and gumption to grandparenting that I shudder with excitement at their potential to influence the course of history simply by loving well: Marie Guise, Janet Youngman Hansen, Patricia Minkove, Chloe and Dave Patten, Suzanne Priscilla Jane Suther, and Jean and George Theisen.

photograph by Amanda Ford

With over 400,000 copies of her titles in print, **Judy Ford** is the hottest new expert on the "art of parenting." Her bestselling titles include *Wonderful Ways to Love a Child, Wonderful Ways to Love a Teen, Wonderful Ways to Be a Family, Expecting Baby* and *Between Mother & Daughter.* She has worked for twenty-nine years with children and families, from gang turf in Los Angeles to crisis intervention in hospitals. A family therapist, she has given seminars on "Parenting with Love and Laughter" to thousands of parents. She lives in Washington with her daughter, Amanda.

To Our Readers

Conari Press, an imprint of Red Wheel/Weiser, publishes books on topics ranging from spirituality, personal growth, and relationships to women's issues, parenting, and social issues. Our mission is to publish quality books that will make a difference in people's lives—how we feel about ourselves and how we relate to one another. We value integrity, compassion, and receptivity, both in the books we publish and in the way we do business.

Our readers are our most important resource, and we value your input, suggestions, and ideas about what you would like to see published. Please feel free to contact us, to request our latest book catalog, or to be added to our mailing list.

Conari Press
An imprint of Red Wheel/Weiser, LLC
500 Third Street, Suite 230
San Francisco, CA 94107
www.redwheelweiser.com